Coachhouse Publ

Pushing
Up The
Daisies

The Famous & Forgotten
on the Isle of Wight

JAN TOMS

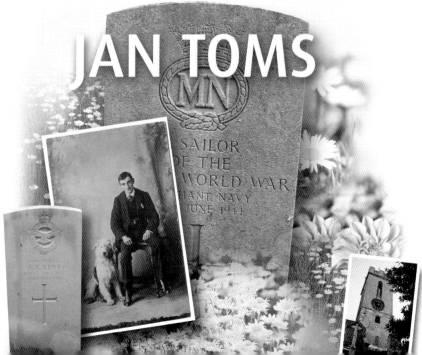

Publishers Details

ISBN: 1-899-392-491
October 2006

Printed in the UK

Published By

Coach House Publications Limited
Isle of Wight, England

The Coach House, School Green Road,
Freshwater, Isle of Wight, PO40 9BB,
Tel: +44 (0) 1983 755655

Further copies of this book and other Island books can be obtained from the publishers by contacting us at the address above or via our online ordering service at:
www.coachhouseonline.co.uk

Book Design by

David Bowles

Contents

Introduction

This book is the tip of a very large iceberg. Almost immediately I realised that I would have to leave out more people than I could include and I regret those omissions.

For every person born and bred here, there are at least two "overners" who left their mark and for every woman, there are perhaps five men – thus history records the past.

Uncovering the people who fill these pages has been a delight. Standing in a churchyard, staring at a name on a gravestone, stepping inside a building where once they stood, seeing the view that they looked upon is its own reward. I feel I have come to know them a little, sometimes to understand and admire if not always to like them.

Geographically the spread is as wide as I could make it. Socially and chronologically they range through time and class. I have tried to be accurate and I apologise for any mistakes I might have made.

In the 17th century Sir John Oglander wrote in his diaries about *"Our Island."* Sometimes I find myself going further and thinking of *"My Island,"* but everyone has his or her own Island, whether coming as a day-tripper, to retire, or being born on these shores. I hope that this small account of those who went before us will add to your enjoyment of this unique and beautiful place.

JAN TOMS

Pushing Up The Daisies

The Famous & Forgotten on the Isle of Wight

For Terry

who trudged around churchyards in the rain,

with love.

Coachhouse Publications Ltd

One
Look Around You

"If you seek his monument,
look around you."

Christopher Wren's epitaph in St Paul's Cathedral

On May 20th 1835 in the dead of night, a coffin was manhandled across the fields from East Cowes Castle to nearby St James's Church. Due for burial the following day, it was rumoured that angry creditors might seize the corpse against outstanding debts. Ensconced within were the mortal remains of 83 year old **John Nash** (1752-1835), architect, self-made gentleman and friend of George IV.

A "little man ...pert, impudent and ugly," he built his reputation as an architect in Wales but his great chance came with plans to develop Marylebone Park in London. Work in Regent Street, Oxford Circus, Piccadilly all bear his mark.

Much of Nash's success came from his friendship with the Prince Regent. How they became close is uncertain. Nash constructed George's fantasy Pavilion at Brighton and when George acceded to the throne Nash represented him over the delicate business of what to do with his troublesome wife, Queen Caroline.

In 1798 John married Mary Ann Bradley, daughter of a coal merchant and more than a quarter of a century his junior (his first wife Jane, from whom he was separated, presumably had died). At about the same time he purchased thirty acres of land on the Isle of Wight with views across the Solent and began work on a castle.

As John's enthusiasm grew, so did his castle, with a tower, turrets, a library, conservatory and numerous rooms. His colleague the landscape gardener Humphrey Repton probably designed the grounds.

John and Mary Ann entertained lavishly and on several occasions the king, who had developed a passion for sailing, stayed. Rumour had it that George also had a passion for Mrs Nash which accounted for their sumptuous life-style.

John added to his empire by purchasing the whole of Ningwood Parish, including the hamlet of Hampstead where he constructed a hunting lodge. Hampstead Grange stands

on the site but virtually nothing remains of the Nash house. One cottage at the farm is said to be to his design. *(above left)*

In 1811 he constructed the Island Institution, standing on the corner of Newport High Street and St James's Square then in 1814 he built the Town Hall, known as the Guildhall, (above right) while for his friend **George Ward**, "an upstart financier of immense wealth," he designed Northwood House at Cowes. *(below left)*

The Wards had moved to the Island on the recommendation of Thomas Arnold's father and George Ward commissioned from Nash the tower at St Mary's Church Cowes as a mausoleum, seventeen members of his family being buried beneath it. Later Wards constructed Weston Manor at Totland complete with chapel and some lie buried in St Saviours churchyard at Totland. *(below right)*

Disaster struck when Nash was persuaded to redesign Buckingham House as a palace. Questions over the spiralling cost were asked, not least concerning Nash's practice of buying raw materials from himself. His reputation suffered and his dream of a baronetcy did not materialise. Instead, he faced increasing debts.

For nearly four decades the Island was Nash's home. One visitor, the painter Joseph Mallard Turner, during several visits produced over one hundred and seventy sketches, many of life at East Cowes Castle.

On Nash's death the castle was sold to pay his debts. Mary Ann moved to the Hampstead lodge, outliving her husband by 16 years. Finally falling into disrepair the castle met the fate of many such monoliths being demolished in the 1960s to make way for a bungalow estate. Only a pillar, a few steps shrouded in bushes, a buried icehouse and a single lodge remain. *(below left)*

As if still expecting to be snatched, John and Mary Ann lie in a tomb just outside the door of St James's Church. *(below right)*

After nearly twenty years of childless marriage Nash cast around for an heir settling on Mary Ann's relatives, the **Pennethornes** five of whom were rumoured to be her natural offspring with George IV.

Mary Ann had adopted her niece **Anne**, a pretty young woman who might have seemed a catch for any aspiring suitor but she remained unmarried, trapped perhaps by her role as companion. Hints of romance with Mr Sewell the curate at St Mildred's Whippingham came to nothing.

When John retired the eldest surviving son **James Pennethorne** became his successor. More fortunate than his benefactor, in 1870, he was knighted.

John Pennethorne who also trained as an architect lived in the Hampstead house along with Anne and their sisters Sarah and Rose. An imposing edifice marks their passing in Shalfleet churchyard. *(page 6)*

While John Nash was entertaining at East Cowes, a newly retired civil engineer was settling into Island life. Although his career did not have the sparkle of Nash, **Daniel Asher Alexander** (1768-1846) had a satisfying list of completed projects to his credit. Employed by Trinity House, he constructed numerous lighthouses and was employed as Surveyor of the London Dock Company but his lasting monument remains the still sinister Dartmoor Prison completed in 1806.

Around 1820 he purchased a house with sea views in Yarmouth High Street then known as the Refuge, which had started life in the 13th century as a hospital. Here Alexander moved with his wife Anna-Maria and their children. Daniel set about adding turrets and battlements to his home, re-naming it The Towers. *(below left)*

From 1827-31 he was secretary to Wellow Baptist church but his sojourn on the Island was overshadowed by tragedy. In 1829, his 19 year-old son Henry died. In tribute to the boy, Daniel donated 30' of height to be added to the church tower at St James's, Yarmouth. (above right) Sadly, Daniel's son William also became ill, dying in 1832, also aged 19. He was buried at the Church of St Mary, Walkhampton Devon, where his elder brother Daniel was a curate.

As with Nash, there was a significant age gap between Anna-Maria Alexander and her husband. Daniel died while visiting Exeter in 1846 and was brought back to Yarmouth for burial. Anna-Maria joined him in 1851. Family plaques in St James's church and a stone set into the floor mark their passing. Their daughter Maria is buried in the churchyard. *(sketch of . Alexander, page 8)*

With the sudden upsurge in 19th century church building, one architect found himself gratifyingly in demand. **Thomas Hellyer** (1811-1894) from Emsworth came to Ryde

possibly on the recommendation of his namesake Phillip who was banker and postmaster in Union Street. By 1851 Thomas was doing well enough to have two live-in servants and an apprentice.

The first church to appear was the Holy Trinity Ryde built between 1840-47. In 1843, work started on St John's Oakfield and concurrently re-building work on the church of the Holy Cross, Binstead. There followed St Peter's Havenstreet (1852), *(opposite page, top right)* St Peter's Seaview (1859) *(opposite page, top left)* and St Saviours at Shanklin.

Hellyer's work was not restricted to the Island. Churches in Leeds, Kingsclere, Alverstoke, Landport and Thatcham were all to his design.

The first two Board Schools in Portsmouth, constructed in red brick, complete with bell towers, opened their doors in January 1873. His other (sadly missed) building on the Island was Ryde County Hospital, in use until 1990.

Thomas married a Portsea girl Harriett Roberts and in 1848 their daughter Harriett was born. By 1861 they had moved into Bouverie House, Melville Street. Thomas must have been pleased to see young Harriet marry in his church at Holy Trinity. In 1889 his wife died and Thomas moved to Elmwood in Queens Road, surviving her by five years. He is interred in a vault in Ryde cemetery.

By their enduring nature, church towers, while no longer essential as lookouts, were useful clock towers when not everyone owned a watch. One such benefactor was **(Theodore) William Spindler**, a German chemist who donated a peal of bells and a clock to St Mary and St Rhadegund, Whitwell. William ran his own newspaper in Berlin and employed 2,000 people in his dye works. He built an estate for his workers, Spindlersfeld that still flourishes. In 1882 he bought the Old Park at St Lawrence in 1882 intending to build a marine town, the remains of which are still discernible in the overgrown roads and beach promenade at Binnel Bay. For his own pleasure he imported about one million Mediterranean trees and shrubs and set about landscaping a superb garden. His drainage scheme had the fortunate effect of stabilising the notoriously landslip-prone area.

Not least of his achievements was the layout of Ventnor Park and the still elegant Park Avenue. Willliam died in 1889, his wife Clara in 1906, both being buried in Whitwell. He was said to preach the *Religion of Humanity*. It is worth taking time to stand inside the church, beneath the tower, to listen to the stately ticking of William's symbol of mortality. *(page 10, top left)*

In similar vein, **Henry Charles Millet R.N.,** a veteran of the Crimean War and churchwarden at St John's Wroxall, presented a clock to the Parish. Born in Wiltshire, during his career as

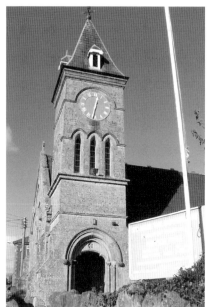

a naval engineer he travelled widely, ending his service at St Catherine's lighthouse before moving to Wroxall where he died in 1909 at the age of 77. A public subscription was set up to raise a tower on St John's Church, suitable to house his clock, completed in 1911. *(above right)*

Equally worthy of remembrance is **William Rayner**, who religiously saved a halfpenny a day to purchase two bells for St Thomas's church at Newport. An ardent campanologist, William died in 1823 and is buried at St George's, Arreton. *(below)*

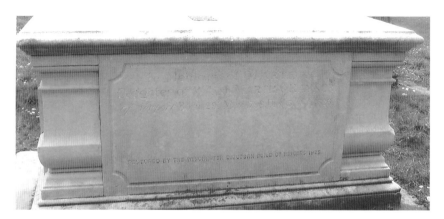

Three Island monuments are hard to ignore. Erected on the high points at Tennyson, St Catherine's and Culver Downs, they celebrate the lives of Lord Tennyson [chapter 3], Michael Hoy and the Earl of Yarborough.

Michael Hoy (1758-1828) was an inspiring example of how determined men might rise from a modest background. His parents were in trade and Michael took advantage of the desire in Russia for luxury goods to set up shop in St Petersburg. In 1786 he was admitted to the Russia Company.

A year later he married Hannah Ramsay who was nearing forty. Whether it was love or advancement that inspired the match, they were together for thirty-five years. In 1797 then living in London, Michael's standing soared when he became an Alderman then a Freeman of the City. In 1812 he was appointed a Sheriff of London and in that year he applied for his own coat of arms.

On the Island he bought up Chale and Walpen Manors and acquired the Hermitage at the foot of St Catherine's Down, no doubt naming it after its famous namesake in St Petersburg.

In 1814, riding high on the defeat of Napoleon, Tsar Alexander the first of Russia made a state visit to England. With his Russian connection Hoy was undoubtedly part of the welcoming entourage. To commemorate the event he erected a 24 metre high monument on the crest of St Catherine's Down. Called the Alexandrian Pillar, it is equally known as the Hoy Monument. A plaque incised on the side reports:

> *In commemoration of the visit of*
> *His Majesty Tsar Alexander I,*
> *Emperor of all the Russias,*
> *to Great Britain in 1814.*
> *In remembrance of many happy years*
> *residence in his dominions*
> *this pillar was erected by Michael Hoy.*

In 1822 Hannah Hoy died and three years later Michael remarried. Like many successful men, his second wife seems to have been much younger and when he died aged seventy he still nursed hopes for an heir. Much of his estate was consigned for her life to Elizabeth. *(page 12 top left & right)*

When the Hoy estate was sold off, the Hermitage and part of St Catherine's Down was bought by **William Henry Dawes** (1808-1863) a military man who had joined the 43rd Regiment of Foot, seeing service in Jamaica. It was not a happy experience for many of his comrades were wiped out by cholera. When he returned to England he retired from the army and settled back on his native Island.

Like many Englishmen, patriotic feelings ran high at the outbreak of the Crimean war. Uncomfortable with the huge pro-Russian erection on his land, Dawes mounted a second plaque on the opposite side of Hoy's pillar, bearing the words:

> *This tablet was erected by William Henry Dawes*
> *late Lieutenant of H.M. 22 Reg.*
> *In honour of those brave men of the allied armies*
> *who fell on the Alma at Inkerman and*
> *at the siege of Sevastopol. AD 1857.*

Unlike Hoy, Dawes was not a self-made man, his fortune being left to him by his infamous Aunt Sophie [Chapter 6]. William is buried in his native St Helens

Inheriting the Appuldurcombe estate at Wroxall was a happy accident for **Charles Anderson Pelham** (1780-1946) as that windfall passed from the last of the Worsleys [chapter 6] to his wife Eleanor. In 1837, the year of Queen Victoria's accession, he acquired the title Earl of Yarborough and Baron Worsley while his daughter Charlotte was a "Woman of the Bedchamber" to the Queen.

The Pelhams came from Lincolnshire, the family seat being at Brocklesby. Charles hung on to Appuldurcombe as it provided a useful base for one of his passions, sailing. In June 1815, at the Thatched House in St James's London, he had founded "The Yacht Club," open only to gentlemen owning a vessel of at least ten tons. Things looked up when the Prince of Wales joined and the epithet "Royal" was added. William IV later amended it to Royal Yacht Squadron.

Pelham died on September 5 1846 aboard his yacht the Kestrel at Vigo in Spain and was succeeded by his son, also Charles. To commemorate his father's "benevolence, kindness... and many virtues, " Charles junior erected a pillar of 341 feet on Culver Down in 1849. Charles senior dispensed largesse, building a quaint school at Godshill and donating to St Lawrence church, while at Wroxall a terrace of houses bears his name. The Appuldurcombe estate was sold in 1855.

On April 21st 1890, **Frank James** (1851-1890) celebrated his 39th birthday by taking part in an elephant shoot. It was to be his last act for a wounded elephant counter-attacked and gored him in the chest. His body was returned home and interred in Kensal Green Cemetery.

As he was a member of the Royal Yacht Squadron, Frank's brothers constructed a home for aged seamen in his memory at Adelaide Grove East Cowes, an ornate brick built structure complete with elaborate chimneys and a tower topped by a gold weather vane. The first residents arrived in time for Christmas 1893.

One of the stipulations was that the building should bear Frank's name and be used for charitable purposes. As the Boer War raged it was converted to nurse injured soldiers. Its third incarnation was as a cottage hospital, formally opened by Princess Beatrice on June 25th 1903.

Sadly, the James Brothers' wish was cut short when the National Health Service decreed that the hospital was no longer modern enough for their purposes and the building was put up for sale. Whether it can survive a 21st century assault remains to be seen. *(below)*

John Hambrough (1794-1863) from Hanwell in Middlesex acquired an estate in Ventnor from Lady Louisa Manners where he demolished most of the buildings and started work on a romantic, castellated construction – Steephill Castle. Sir Joseph Paxton who designed the Crystal Palace declared that having travelled from Stockholm to Constantinople: *"never have I seen anything as beautiful as this."*

Hambrough was closely involved in the rapid development of Ventnor, endowing both the newly built St Catherine's church and the local schools.

Alas, he was not to see his Steephill masterpiece because before it was completed he went blind. He also suffered the loss of his eldest son Albert, a natural historian who, while staying at Steephill in 1861, was carried off by a gastric illness.

John died on February 4th 1863 to be followed only ten days later by his wife Sophia, both being interred at St Catherine's. Like East Cowes Castle, Steephill gave way to a housing estate. *(below)*

Two
Let Battle Commence

"To save your world,
you asked this man to die:
Would this man,
could he see you now, ask why?"

W H Auden

A plaque at the High Street/Esplanade junction at Seaview records the last invasion of the Island by French troops. A small fort at Nettlestone was destroyed on July 21st 1545 but in a similar landing at Bonchurch the French forces were repulsed.

One version of this event comes from **Sir John Oglander** (1585 - 1655). Although not a military man per se, his *Royalist Notebook* gives a flavour of the times in which he lived:

On May 10 1627 one thousand soldiers, *"being Sir Alexander Brett's regiment"* were billeted on the Island. At first Sir John feared that there would be insufficient food but happily that was not the case and he concludes: *"... seeing we were well paid for their board [we] could have been content on the same conditions to have kept them longer."*

Not so six months later when fifteen hundred "Scotch" soldiers arrived when the plan to ship them to the Ile de Re was abandoned. Sir John complained that their officers, although described as gentlemen *"knew not how to cut bread or meat."* Discipline broke down and these unintelligible aliens terrorised the natives, *"committing divers murders"* and other crimes. One wonders how many natives still have a hint of Scottish blood in their veins?

There being no standing army, Sir John recorded an unfortunate incident following a muster on St George's Down at Newport. Having given the order to fire a last volley, he reports that *"Sampson Saphior, a young fellow and pretty shopman... was hit in the poll* of the head." Although there was no evidence of a wound, he died. Sir John concluded that *"all the nerves and sinews in the poll of his head were either broken off or, with the fire, shrunk up and his brain turned in his head."*

The Oglanders arrived at Brading by the 12th century. With their Norman connections they settled comfortably into Island life, relinquishing this heritage eight hundred years later.

In St Mary's church Brading, three generations are remembered in wood. Sir William Oglander who was born in 1554, married Ann Dillington of Knighton Gorges. Rarely for the Dillingtons this was a happy marriage, producing Sir John who made a priceless contribution to history with his diary.

A supporter of Charles 1st he was imprisoned and left an "as it happens" account, culminating in the King's arrival at Carisbrooke Castle. One gets the impression of a decent man, increasingly pained by events but maintaining his own standards against the odds.

Sir John suffered two tragedies both caused by smallpox. In 1632 his adored son George, newly down from Oxford and touring Paris, was struck down by the disease. He was 23. In 1643, while Sir John was languishing in gaol his beloved wife went to London to try to secure his release only to contract the same illness. He never recovered from these losses. A monument to young George is in St Mary's, Brading.

For his effigy, Sir John adopted a nonchalant pose, reclining on his side, his chin supported on his hand and his feet crossed. *(below)*

The black carved bust of Charles 1st in St Nicholas's chapel Carisbrooke, exhorts the viewer to: "**Remember** " - although exactly what, it does not say. *(above)* In coming to the Island Charles made a grave mistake but for no one was it more disastrous than the newly appointed governor **Robert Hammond** (1621-54).

Hammond came from Chertsey, a second son of good family, his grandfather being physician to James 1st. At the outbreak of the Civil War, Robert's Uncle Henry was chaplain to the King while his godfather the Earl of Essex was leader of the parliamentary forces. Robert threw in his lot with Essex.

During the following five years he fought in numerous battles, was taken prisoner and killed a fellow soldier in a duel. By the age of 26 he was a colonel in the New Model Army but by then he was battle weary and disillusioned. He asked to be relieved of his commission.

Both army and Parliament recognised his qualities. His resignation was refused and he was appointed Captain and Governor of the Isle of Wight, an undemanding post that would allow him to recover from the stresses of war. One can imagine his relief, stepping ashore at Cowes on Monday 13th September 1647. He may have visited before as his Aunt Jane Dingley lived at Wolverton while his cousin Robert was the minister at Brighstone.

A life of relaxation beckoned but weeks after his arrival the king, panicked by threats of murder by his guards, ran away. Perhaps the fact that his chaplain's nephew was the Captain made him choose the Island as his refuge. Robert, seeking obscurity, was thrust onto the centre stage of English politics.

For nearly a year he was first host then gaoler to the king, juggling the conflicting demands of army and parliament, struggling to keep Charles safe but contained, fighting off the paparazzi and keeping the curious at bay. Meanwhile the king's intransigence made it ever more difficult as he orchestrated a series of failed escapes. Robert was eventually lured to the mainland and in his absence Charles was transported to London to his trial and execution.

Robert returned to relative obscurity, becoming an MP for Reading then being appointed by Cromwell to the Irish Council. Within two months of reaching Dublin he succumbed to a fever and died. He was thirty-three.

Robert's physical legacy is the bowling green at Carisbrooke Castle made to keep his difficult prisoner amused. Cousin Robert Dingley, a writer and proponent of religious reform, lies beneath the chancel of Brighstone Church.

In one of life's small ironies, **Sir Faithful Fortescue** (1581-1666), laid to rest at St Mary's Carisbrooke on May 29 1666, is remembered for an act of treachery.

Faithful was born in Devon having all the right credentials for a military career. As a young man he went to Ireland to command a regiment of foot under his uncle, Sir Arthur Chichester. At the age of 25 he was Constable of Carrickfergus Castle and before he was 30, he was knighted.

In 1641 Faithful served as Governor of Drogheda. The long-suffering Irish rebelled and in the ensuing siege, two of his sons were killed. He was placed under the command of the Earl of Essex and when in 1642 King Charles raised his standard at Nottingham signalling the start of civil war Faithful found himself fighting on what he considered to be the wrong side.

At the first major battle at Edgehill, Faithful made contact with Charles's nephew Prince Rupert declaring that he and his men would defect to the Royalist Camp. Unfortunately, in the heat of battle they forgot that they were still wearing the orange sashes of the Parliamentarians and seventeen were killed.

As the king's cause looked increasingly hopeless, Faithful, back in Ireland, had a choice between joining the Protestant Parliamentarians or the mainly Catholic Royalists. He chose the former.

1651 found him in Stirling with Charles II. When Charles was defeated at the battle of Worcester, Faithful fled with him to the Continent. After the restoration he returned to London with the King until 1665 when the outbreak of plague made it sensible to leave. He came to the Isle of Wight to stay with his friend Sir William Stephens [See Chapter 7] at Bowcombe Manor where he died shortly afterwards at the age of 85.

Two hundred years later, Lord Clermont erected a plaque in St Mary's Carisbrooke recording his noble ancestor's life. *(below)*

In 1793 hundreds of soldiers from **Hesse**, now in modern day Germany, were shipped off to confront the newly fledged French Republic. They had no idea of the horror that awaited them at the hands of their English Allies.

The planned landing in France did not materialise so they arrived at Spithead on January 4th 1794, the ships crowded with men and horses. A shock awaited them. Because they were foreigners they were not permitted to land.

The first to suffer were the horses and within two weeks eighty-three had died. Reluctantly the remainder were taken off accompanied by grooms who had to supply their own food. It was another five weeks before they were even found beds.

On board ship an infectious illness broke out. By February 21st 641 men were sick but another week passed before they were grudgingly accommodated ashore in makeshift storerooms. Requests for somewhere draught-proof and heated were ignored. Between February 4th and May 2nd, 82 men and two women died.

As with most military blunders, accusations flew back and forth, aimed mainly at the Duke of York who had requested the men in such numbers. Those who survived finally departed on April 2nd to continue the battle against the French. The dead were buried in Whippingham churchyard, their bones discovered when a wall was re-aligned. Although re-interred, their final resting-place is unknown. In 1906 a plaque in marble and alabaster was placed in the church acknowledging their sacrifice. A list of those who died is held in Whippingham Visitor Centre. *(below)*

Several Victoria Cross winners are commemorated in Island churchyards. The award was instituted in 1856 but given retrospectively to those who carried out acts of valour since the start of the Crimean War (1854). The medal is still forged by Hancocks the jewellers in Burlington Arcade London from the bronze of cannons captured from the Russians at Sebastapol.

Willam Thomas Rickard (1828-1905) served as quartermaster with the Royal Navy on the HMS Weser. On October 11 1855 William went to destroy quantities of forage stored by the Russians on the shore of the Sivash, a saltwater lagoon in Southern Ukraine.

Although under fire he and his companions succeeded in setting light to the store and began the hazardous return journey. A fellow seaman collapsed, sinking into the mud and was unable to free himself and although exhausted, Rickard returned to help him. On reaching their ship they learned that the fodder store had burned to the ground.

After the war Rickard joined the Coastguard Service, rising to the rank of Chief Officer. He married and raised three children at Smallbrook, near Ryde and is buried in Ryde Cemetery. His funeral was something of an occasion, the body being conveyed through the streets in an open hearse. Thirty sailors from Portsmouth wearing straw hats and black armbands lined St James's church, the Volunteer Band accompanied the cortege and The Last Post was played at the graveside.

In 1857 **Major Henry Tombs** (1825-1874) served with the Bengal Horse Artillery at the time of the Indian Mutiny. On July 9th 1857 during the siege of Delhi twice he went to the rescue of a junior officer, on each occasion killing his assailant.

Tombs came from a family steeped in military service. He was born at sea on November 10 1824 en route to Calcutta and in 1839 entered the East India Company's military college. Thereafter he was present at numerous engagements throughout the sub-continent. Lord Roberts described him as an unusually handsome man and a thorough soldier, also observing that he was *"more feared than liked by his men until they realised what a grand leader he was."*

Known as Sir Harry, Tombs later received the KCB and was promoted to the rank of Major General. On March 1 1869 he married Georgina Janet Stirling, daughter of an admiral and twenty years his junior. He died on August 2nd 1874 at Newport and is buried in Mount Joy Cemetery.

A month after Tombs' heroic action, **Colonel Henry George Gore Browne** (1830-1912), serving with the 32nd Regiment (later Duke of Cornwall's Light Infantry) at Lucknow, came to the rescue of the British Residency which for five months had been under siege, pinned down by two heavy guns. Browne leapt into the battery and spiked the guns. Born in County Roscommon he retired to Shanklin where he died on November 15 1912 being buried at St Mary the Virgin, Brook.

A year later, **Sir Samuel James Browne** (1824-1901), son of John Browne of the East India Company's medical service, was in charge of the 2nd Punjab cavalry at Lucknow. He and his men carried out numerous raids on rebel groups culminating in a surprise attack at Sirpur in Hyderabad where at considerable risk to himself, Browne charged almost single-handed, preventing the enemy gunners from reloading. During this attack his left arm was severed and he was twice injured in the knee. Following the loss of his arm he designed a belt to facilitate carrying his sword, the name *Sam Browne* coming into regular military parlance.

Browne married Lucy Sherwood whose father was in the East India Company's medical service. He was ultimately promoted to General. He retired to Ryde living at The Wood, St John's Park where he died on 14 March 1901. He was cremated and his ashes buried at Ryde Cemetery.

St Mary's churchyard Brighstone hosts a commemorative headstone to **Lieutenant George Albert Cairns VC** (1913-1944), erected by his parents.

Cairns was born in London and during the Second World War went with the Somerset Light Infantry (Prince Albert's) attached to the South Staffordshire Regiment, to the Far East. Promoted to the rank of lieutenant, on March 5th 1944 George and his comrades were dropped into Burma (Myanmar) by glider, their task being to block the Japanese lines of communication. On March 13th George found himself at Henu Block where, during a Japanese attack, an enemy officer hacked off his arm with a sword. Grabbing the man's weapon George killed him and made a frenzied counter-attack, wiping out several of his adversaries before collapsing from his wounds. His action so inspired his companions that what might have been a rout turned into a victory.

In May 1949, King George VI awarded him a posthumous VC. *(opposite page)*

In stark and ironic contrast to the above, the death of a young soldier at Fort Victoria deserves remembrance if only for the cruel circumstances in which he met his end.

On the Friday before Christmas 1889, 24 year-old **Sapper Andrew Templar's** coffin was carried from Golden Hill Fort to Yarmouth. The Oxfordshire Light Infantry Band played Beethoven's Funeral March accompanied by muffled drums and his fellow soldiers carried him to his last resting-place. As the bitter easterly wind blew over the bareheaded mourners, a volley of blank fire rang out and the men said their final goodbyes.

Andrew seems to have been born at Ludgershall in Buckinghamshire but then moved to London, starting an apprenticeship as a carpenter. Perhaps the glamour of army life seemed more inviting, which found him based at Fort Victoria - and the circumstances of his sudden death? While putting up the Christmas decorations in the Fort mess room, he fell and was accidentally killed.

Visit any village, walk into any churchyard and you come face to face with a reminder of the sacrifice made by those lost in two world wars. There being too many to include it is hoped that those mentioned will represent their fellows.

IN
EVERLASTING MEMORY OF
OUR DEARLY BELOVED SON
Lieut. GEORGE A. CAIRNS v.c
SOMERSET L.I.F. (WYNGATE'S CHINDITS)
KILLED IN ACTION, BURMA MARCH 1944,
TWICE MENTIONED IN DESPATCHES
AWARDED THE VICTORIA CROSS
(POSTHUMOUSLY) MAY 1946

Starting with two local lowly men, **Albert Edward Kent** (1900-1919) was born at Shanklin, the middle child in a family of nine. His father Frederick was a carpenter who built numerous houses around Shanklin having a short period of success before he over-stretched himself.

Bert enrolled as a private in the Royal Air Force. The lure of this new, glamorous force is easy to imagine but he died at home on July 22nd 1919, aged 19 years, a casualty of war.

How did the family cope with this sad outcome, his mother's tears, the grieving of his siblings, his father hiding his hurt? Was there too perhaps a sweetheart, secretly nursing her loss? If so, like Bert, she was long ago consigned to obscurity. *(opposite & below left)*

Edwin Lewis (1889 – 1918) was a Lake man. In 1913 he married Maggie Kent (Bert's sister) at St Paul's Church Shanklin, going to live in New Village, Freshwater where he worked as a boot mender at Golden Hill Fort. At about this time Maggie sent her sister Nell a photograph of them both, smiling, exuding an air of contentment.

Edwin joined the Hampshire Regiment, 2nd Battalion and was posted to Northern France. There he died on May 29th 1918, one of 226 casualties identified in the cemetery at Cinq Rues, Hazebrouk. There were no children and Maggie never remarried. *(below right)*

Both Bert and Edwin are incised on the war memorial at Shanklin, two out of the 107 Shanklin men recorded as killed during World War One. Bert's grave is in Shanklin cemetery and a diamond shaped stone to Edwin records Maggie's loss. *(Shanklin war memorial, page 26 top right)*

Unlike Albert Kent and Edwin Lewis, **Hugh Edward Richard Boxer DSO** (1871-1915) came from a family steeped in military derring-do. Hugh's great grandfather, Rear Admiral Sir Edward died of cholera at Balaclava Harbour having been called back into service when he was seventy. His grandfather, also Edward, was a major general, while his own father, Lt General Edward Boxer, died four months before Hugh's birth when his ship HMS Captain foundered off Finisterre. Hugh's elder brother, another Edward who died aged 32, had the unusual third forename of Shrapnel.

At Thorpe Lodge, The Broadway, Sandown on June 21 1915, Hugh's wife Jeannie received a telegram reporting him wounded and missing. He was last seen in command of the 1st Battalion Lincolnshire Regiment at Hooge.

For six months she advertised for information, clinging to the belief that he may have survived but in January 1916 the German authorities reported that his body, along with twenty of his men, had been found. They were buried near to the place where they had fallen.

Earlier in his career his foot had been shattered by a Dervish bullet, leaving him permanently lame. At the age of 55 Jeannie committed suicide at a nursing home in Weymouth.

Hugh is remembered on a bronze memorial plaque and in two stained glass windows at Christ Church, Sandown.

In death as in life the status of the deceased is remembered. At St Olave's church Gatcombe is an imposing tomb to **Charles Grant Seely** (1894-1917), eldest son of Charles the 2nd Baronet and Dame Hilda his wife. Charles attended Eton then Cambridge and on the outbreak of war joined the Isle of Wight Rifles. The inscription on his tomb tells us that having served with distinction in the Gallipoli and Egyptian campaigns, *"he fell gloriously, thrice wounded at Gaza on April 19 1917,"* where he is buried.

His memorial was commissioned from Sir Thomas Brock who created Queen Victoria's imposing monument outside Buckingham Palace. A formal unveiling took place on October 2nd 1922 carried out by Princess Beatrice. Perhaps unfortunately for Charles, Gatcombe is within easy distance of the former mental asylum of Whitecroft and one of the patients later attacked the sculpture defacing Charles's nose.

The Seely family were in the mid-19th century Lincolnshire coal mine owners, becoming part of the Island gentry, representing the Wight in Parliament. The Charles Seely who originally purchased Brooke House invited the freedom fighter Giuseppe Garibaldi to the

Island where in 1864 he planted trees at Brooke House and Farringford. "Jack" Seely, 1st Baron Mottistone, uncle of the war hero Charles, who resided at Mottistone Manor, won renown for his service throughout World War One, immortalising his horse Warrior in a biography. The Seely name lives on in the former Library in Node Hill Newport, which they founded. *(opposite page, top left)*

On a hill at Havenstreet stands a shrine to **Richard Thomas Cyril Willis Fleming** of Binstead. On August 4th 1918, the day after his 24th birthday, Richard was killed by a Turkish airman. His parents extended the memorial to include all the war dead of the parish. During the Second World War, Major Everard Leach an American pilot was killed nearby and his name added to the memorial. The building houses an altar behind a screen, the land is consecrated and members of the Willis Fleming family still use the site for cremated burials. *(below)*

There cannot be many husbands and wives inscribed on village war memorials.

In each of their ways, the **Gartside Tippings** (Died 1915 and 1917) were unique – Henry was the oldest officer serving in the navy, whilst Mary was awarded the Croix de Guerre, specifically re-instated for women after she was shot on active service by a deranged French soldier.

Henry was born in Dublin in 1849 the son of Gartside Gartside Tipping and at the age of 12 was a naval cadet in Portsmouth. Mary was born in Blackburn in 1867, her father being Captain Flynn of the Royal Artillery. They married in 1890 when Henry was 41 and Mary 23. From his uncle the Reverend Vernon Tipping he inherited Quarrwood, a large house at Binstead and here they were living in 1901 along with their three children, four servants and a governess. The war changed everything. Henry, who was retired, answered the call to arms joining the Mercantile Marine Reserve as Lieutenant

Commander aboard the armed yacht Sanda. On September 25 1915, she was fired on by shore batteries off Zeebrugge and lost.

Mary, widowed at 47, took work in the canteen of the Munitions factory at Woolwich. In January 1917 she joined the Women's Emergency Corps, an unlikely mixture of conventional, well to do women and radical feminists.

Perhaps the death of her husband decided her to volunteer for active service, which found her in a French war zone on March 14 1917 when she was killed. A requiem mass was said for her at Berkeley Square.

A brief mention for **John, Earl Jellicoe** (1859-1935), Admiral of the Fleet, First Sea Lord and Governor General of New Zealand, remembered for his command of the Grand Fleet at the battle of Jutland (1916). This decisive World War One naval battle left a legacy of controversy but ultimately British superiority at sea was established. During a long naval career, Jellicoe served in China where he was shot in the chest and carried the bullet inside him for the rest of his life. Being a sometime resident of St Lawrence Hall, on his death a memorial plaque was erected in Bonchurch church where he worshipped. *(below left)*

August 12 1915 was a bad day for the Island. **Edward, Frederick and William Urry** aged 35, 21 and 26, brothers serving with the same battalion and Edward's brother in law, **William Richardson** aged 21 all died in the Suvla Bay operation at Gallipoli. Their sacrifice is recorded on the Newport War Memorial and the Island Memorial in St Nicholas Church, Carisbrooke.

On the same day, **Clayton and Donald Ratsey** (29 and 31) brothers and captains in the 1/8th Isle of Wight Rifles, Princess Beatrice's Battalion were killed. Neither has a known grave but their names appear on the Helles Memorial to the missing. Their brother **Lt Stephen Ratsey**, aged 24 of the same regiment, died on April 19 at Gaza and is buried there. The sons of Thomas and Lucy, the sail making family of Cowes, they are commemorated on a plaque in St Mary's church, Cowes.

A memorial to those who died at Gallipoli stands at Heroes Corner at Mount Joy Cemetery. *(opposite page, right)*

Several Island families suffered the loss of more than one member.

In Newport Cemetery the familiar Imperial War Graves Commission headstones mark the graves of **Henry and William Quantrill** the sons of Henry and Ada of Newport. Three decades after their deaths, Henry senior, then 89 years of age, was laid to rest with William followed by Ada who was buried with her elder boy Henry. The old couple waited half a lifetime to be reunited with their sons. *(below left & right)*

Those who were able to do so assuaged the pain of loss by erecting a memorial. Following the deaths of her sons **Stanley and Harold Jackson Snowden**, their mother donated a stained glass window to St Peter's church at Seaview. Stanley, a captain in the Middlesex Regiment and Harold, serving with the Royal Flying Corps, died within five months of each other. *(page 30, top left)*

When **Lt Commander Christopher Ellis** died at the very end of the war, his father the

minister of Holy Trinity Church Ryde must have felt relief that his son **Paul**, also serving with the navy, had survived. In a bitter blow, Paul, in command of a submarine, perished when the vessel was accidentally sunk on January 10th 1924. Brass plaques in Holy Trinity recall their loss.

Colonel Mark and Mrs Isabel Goldie commissioned a marble plaque depicting St George to be erected in Shorwell Church to their sons **Mark**, a major in the Royal Artillery and **Amyas**, serving with the Worcester Regiment. Mark lies in Aire Cemetery France with nearly one thousand others, while Amyas is recorded with more than twenty thousand casualties at the Helles Memorial in Greece. Their memorial at Shorwell states: *"Nature might stand up and say to all the world that these were men." (above right)*

Commuting along the Forest Road, negotiating the traffic calming and obeying the speed restrictions, one gives little thought to **Parkhurst Military Cemetery**. The gates stand closed and there is a sense of exclusion. Inside however are nearly 200 burials, a quiet sadness reflecting this aspect of Island history.

Men were posted to the Island from all corners of the British globe. In death, soldiers from the Warwickshire and Cornwall regiments rub shoulders with men from Jersey,

Ireland, Canada and Australia. Perhaps the most poignant graves are those of unknown soldiers with their simple epitaph *"known only to God." (page 31. top left)*

Nor are the graves restricted to servicemen. Among the tombstones are those to **Jacqueline Sara Picton**, *"our little darling,"* who died on her 8th birthday, 13th October 1937. (above, right) Robert and Agnes Lees of the 2nd Battalion Scottish Rifles suffered the death of their baby son **Archibald Wallace**, aged only 9 months, *(next page. top left)* while Quarter Master William Oliphant lost both his wife Margaret in March 1896 and a year later, his thirty month old daughter **Kathleen Mia**. *(next page. top right)* The enemy is not only on the battlefield. *(next page. bottom left)*

An unusual drinking trough dedicated *"To the horses and dogs who also bore the burden and heat of the day 1914-1920"* stands beside the war memorial at the top of the Fairway, Lake. On the reverse side it entreats: *"Be ye merciful. (next page. bottom right)*

Although military casualties were proportionately less in World War II, with the advent of aerial bombardments, civilian losses increased. Nowhere is this more graphically illustrated than in East and West Cowes.

The night of 4/5 May 1942 was one of hell. Cowes residents had grown used to the careless dropping of odd bombs by German fighters. When the sirens began around eleven on May 4th there was no reason to think it would be any different but before dawn the towns had endured two attacks by 160 German planes. More than 70 people lay dead and whole families had been wiped out.

The youngest to die was little **Peter Vivian Coster**, just five weeks, who perished with his mother and 13 year old sister. Nine-month old **Vivienne Cooke** along with her two sisters and brother plus both parents also lost their lives. The oldest to die was 82

year old **Ellen Varney**, while **William and Naomi Broadwater**, with a combined age of 155, perished together after 42 years of marriage.

Because of the scale of loss there were communal graves in Northwood Cemetery and Kingston Road (East Cowes) *(above left & right)* both marked by large tablets recording the dead. Other commemorations include one to four members of the ARP who perished that night, at St James Church East Cowes.

Things might have been worse had not the Polish ship **Blyskawica** (Lightning) been undergoing a refit at J Samuel White's shipyard. She kept up a bombardment and smokescreen to force the planes higher. A grateful population saw the erection of memorial plaques on the fortieth, fiftieth and sixtieth anniversaries of this tragedy in a shelter along the Parade at Cowes. In 2004 an area was named after the Polish Commander Francki.

Two men brought prosperity and danger to East and West Cowes. **John Samuel White's** shipyard had been active in Cowes since 1802. Over the next 150 years its production spread to both sides of the river Medina and ranged from building lifeboats to warships, cranes to aircraft, at its height employing up to 3,500 men. No wonder it was a target for the Luftwaffe. J Samuel is buried in a now overgrown grave at Kingston Road cemetery in East Cowes. Further along the Medina **Samuel Saunders** developed a light, waterproof plywood ideal for building speedboats and seaplanes. From his Folly workshop the Princess flying boat emerged.

Samuel lived at Padmore House, Whippingham with his wife Kate. On the death of his daughter Ethel, he designed her a boat shaped coffin. Samuel is buried in Whippingham churchyard, his grave sporting marine dolphins. *(page 34, top left)*

Unusually 19 year-old **John Wilson Cawte**, a server at All Saints Church Godshill, who died at Normandy in 1944 is remembered by a painted statue of St George in the church. Perhaps it is carved in young John's likeness? *(page 34, top right)*

Mrs Ida Mary Salter of Vernham's Dean in Hampshire was able to make a unique and beautiful gesture in remembrance of her only son **Edward Talfourd Salter** who died in Italy on October 13 1943. While he lies far from home in the Cassino War Cemetery, a spectacular swathe of land stretching west from Compton Bay was donated to the National Trust in his memory. A cairn set with beach pebbles marks his sacrifice. *(opposite page)*

Apart from the ubiquitous war memorials, an assortment of unusual commemorations are to be found. In Colwell Heath Lane, Freshwater are a pair of bungalows constructed to accommodate ex-servicemen from both world wars while at St Olaves, Gatcombe, a heating system was installed in remembrance of members of the Isle of Wight Rugby Club. A seat in St James's churchyard Yarmouth commemorates women who died while serving in the Auxiliary Territorial Service and a spinney at Mornington Green Cowes known as Jenny's Wood commemorates the WRNS who served at HMS Vectis, a landing craft base for combined operations training, at Seaview. The wood was dedicated by Countess Mountbatten on May 8th 1995.

Three
Creative Genius?

"Come not when I am dead,
To drop thy foolish tears
upon my grave"

Alfred Lord Tennyson

The poet and novelist **John Sterling** (1806-1844) may well have been forgotten but for the passion of his biographer Thomas Carlyle who remembered him as a *"beautiful and cheerful"* man with an *"ever flowing wealth of ideas."*

John intended to study law but the lure of ideas and literature captivated him. He was strongly influenced by his tutor at Trinity College Cambridge, Julius Hare a clergyman.

In 1830 he married Susannah Barton, according to Carlyle *"a graceful, pious-minded, honourable and affectionate woman."* What should have been an idyllic episode was overshadowed by the onset of tuberculosis and for months he was confined to the sick room. Having inherited a share in a sugar estate in St Vincent, they travelled there. A few months after their arrival, their first son was born.

John found St Vincent fascinating. On the subject of slaves, his initial impression was that they were *"decidedly unfit for freedom."* This changed following a hurricane when he saw them as *"Heroes of Antiquity, risking their lives and limbs for us..."*

The climate did not suit Susan and after fifteen months they came home. John hoped to persuade the government to introduce universal education for the slaves as a prelude to emancipation. When this failed he took the advice of his friend Samuel Taylor Coleridge and went to Germany.

Encouraged by Julius Hare, now rector at Hurstmonceux in Sussex he took Holy Orders. As curate to Hare, he threw himself into his role but something was missing. Using his poor health as an excuse, after only eight months he moved to London.

In 1833 his first novel *Arthur Coningsby* was published, the semi-autobiographical adventures of a young man. As with his poetry, it made little impression.

Driven by increasing ill health, by 1840 he was spitting blood. Now began a period of nomadic existence travelling each winter to the Continent. He spent that of 1842 in Naples.

Returning to his family at Falmouth, tragedy struck. John's mother was in poor health. He was torn between the desire to visit her or to stay with Susan who was about to give birth. On Good Friday Susan was delivered of a daughter but by Easter Monday her health gave cause for concern. In the post John received news that his mother had died. Reluctantly he told Susan who said: *"poor man,"* thinking of John's father. They were her last words for in two hours she too was dead.

The bereaved man moved to the gentler climate of Ventnor taking a house, Hillside, in Mitchell Avenue.

At Falmouth he had met the diarist Caroline Fox, niece of Charles James Fox, an "aristocratic outsider." In January 1844 he proposed marriage but she turned him down. It was soon clear that he was fading and in September of that year he died.

John left his papers jointly to Julius Hare and Thomas Carlyle. Carlyle disliked Hare's biography and produced his own. John is buried in the old cemetery of Bonchurch. *(previous page, middle, bottom left & right)*

A terracotta plaque on a large brick house in Birmingham Road, Cowes marks the birthplace of **Thomas Arnold** (1795-1847) the reforming headmaster at Rugby School. Thomas's father William was collector of customs at East Cowes, also postmaster a role taken over by his wife on his death when Thomas was six. William is buried at Whippingham along with his son Matthew who in 1820 drowned in the Solent. Thereafter the family left the Island.

Thomas, precocious, learned but sociable, was ordained a deacon in 1818 but certain religious doubts, plus a desire to marry, kept him from the priesthood. Having run a school at Laleham along the Thames he was in 1827 appointed headmaster of Rugby.

English public school education was at an all time low. Poor teaching, drunkenness and bullying were rife. Arnold focussed on the Sixth Form, instilling in his charges a sense that they would be judged by their actions. He was accused of preaching revolution and not being fit to have charge of boys but the memory of his passion stayed with many and changes for the better ensued.

In 1820 Thomas married Mary Penrose with whom he was idyllically happy and had eleven children. He took a house in the Lake District where he became a close friend of William Wordsworth.

In 1836 he paid a visit to the Island being touched by the beauty he remembered from childhood.

Thomas wrote numerous books including a three-volume work on the History of Rome. His own biography was written by Dean Stanley but it was a work of fiction "Tom Brown's Schooldays," that kept the school and its reforms forever in the minds of those who followed. *(opposite page, top left)*

'...But the sea, Jack, the sea – the little waterfall – then the white cliffs – then St Catherine's Hill....' It would be hard not to be caught up in the breathless enthusiasm of the poet John Keats as he described the view from Shanklin Chine, written in April 1817 to his "affectionate friend" **John Hamilton Reynolds** (1794-1852).

Perhaps it was this long remembered passion, long after Keats died that drove Reynolds to seek sanctuary in the Island.

Reynolds was born on September 9 1794 in Shrewsbury. Later his family moved to

London and on leaving school he worked first as a clerk in a newspaper office then for an insurance firm.

At the same time he pursued his passion for writing poetry and in 1814 his verse *Safie: an Eastern Tale* was published. He had unashamedly copied Byron's style and to his delight the great Lord George liked it. Other work followed with sufficient success to allow John to give up paid work. Around this time he met Keats and the two men collaborated on poetic works.

By 1817 though, Reynolds had fallen in love and the prospect of marriage forced him to find a more secure income. Through the help of his friend James Rice he became articled to a firm of solicitors. He continued to write poetry and even a "comic drama" that was performed for seven weeks at the English Opera House. His best known poem *Peter Bell* was published during this time.

Completing his legal training, on August 31 1822 he married Eliza Powell Drewe and three years later a daughter, Lucy was born. John continued to combine legal work with writing and although he had some success with both, his interest in the law waned and in 1835, when Lucy died aged only ten, his career took a sharp dive. Drinking heavily, depressed, he resigned his post and moved with Eliza to Newport, taking a house at 36 Node Hill. (above left, bottom) He found a post as assistant clerk to the county court, working there until he died on November 15 1852. He was buried at Church Litten, his tombstone being one of few still remaining on the former cemetery that once accommodated Elizabethan plague victims. *(previous page, top right)*

In 1902, a bibliophile named Thomas Greenwood righted what he felt to be a long overdue wrong. Known as the "Apostle of the Library Movement," Greenwood paid for the erection of a red marble monument over the grave of **Edward Edwards** (1812-1885), lying neglected since 1886 in Niton churchyard.

Edward's grandfather was a labourer in Whitechapel. His father Anthoney [sic] improved himself sufficiently to run his own bricklaying business, taking Edward as an apprentice but in 1832 he went bankrupt. Raised with the ethic of self-improvement, Edward devoted himself to his neglected schooling having a moment of supreme satisfaction when he obtained a reader's ticket for the British Museum, the only free library in London. In 1838 he secured a post as temporary library assistant. The British Museum probably got more than it bargained for and Edward began a sustained campaign to secure free library access across the country, a concept firmly resisted in some quarters, but in 1850 the Public Libraries Act became law. Manchester was one of the first towns to enforce the act and Edwards was appointed chief librarian of the Manchester Free Library. His radicalism however led to disagreements and in 1859 he resigned.

At the age of 31 he fell in love with Margaretta Hayward, aged 40. Despite family disapproval (the age gap plus his lack of prospects), the couple married. Edward immersed himself in writing serious tomes on library related topics.

He and Margaretta became peripatetic. One of their venues was the Isle of Wight and after Margaretta's death, Edward moved here permanently renting a room at Sea View House in Niton with a widow, Mrs Mary Jane Musson. He may have entertained ideas of a more permanent relationship but Mary Jane married Thomas Dunford a retired butler and for a while the three inhabited the same house.

Edward's prospects remained modest. From his pension of £80 a year from the Civil List, he supported his sister Elizabeth. Immersed in revising his *Handbook of Literature and Collective Biography,* in mid July 1885 he visited Freshwater Gate. When he returned to Niton a shock awaited him. Owing £30 in back rent, Mr Dunford took the opportunity of evicting him. His belongings were scattered outside, all except his books which were held in lieu of rent.

Edward was now 73. As he wandered aimlessly he met the Reverend John Harrison and explained his difficulty. At home, Mrs Harrison was about to give birth but with true Christian charity, John took him home, sending a handcart to collect his belongings. Edward settled into The Manse as a non-paying guest, borrowing the vicar's reference books the better to accommodate his studies.

In November a bill of exchange fell due from a wine merchant in Ventnor. Edward could not pay. The following morning he went out early and did not return. It was bitterly cold and he was eventually located lying frost bitten in the roofless "Salt Cellar" on St Catherine's Down. The Harrisons nursed him back to health then persuaded him to move into St Catherine's Lodge nearby.

On February 6 1886, Edward retired to bed early and when he failed to appear the next morning, his landlady, Mrs Wheeler found that he had died in his sleep. He was buried in Niton churchyard. His sister Elizabeth hung on to life for another eleven years. *(above left & right)*

When young **Alfred Tennyson's** grandmother died, he wrote a poem for which his grandfather gave him half a sovereign with the words: *"That is the first money my boy you've made by poetry – and take my word for it – it will be the last!"*

Tennyson (1809-1892) was born in Lincolnshire, one of twelve children of a clever but melancholic clergyman. With his brothers Frederick and Charles he early started writing verse. They offered their first efforts to a local bookseller who paid them £20.

At Trinity College Cambridge, Alfred met Charles Hallam who became his closest friend. Hallam's early death shook him greatly and he spent seventeen years composing a 200 page long tribute, *In Memoriam,* seeking to work through his grief and restore his religious faith. The poem was nearly lost when he left it in a cupboard.

These were dark times. When his second volume of poems was badly reviewed, Alfred published nothing for ten years. At his brother Charles's wedding he met the bride's sister Emily Sellwood. They became engaged but Alfred's precarious finances caused him to break it off. Then, in 1850 everything changed. *In Memoriam* was published to instant success and as Wordsworth had died that year, the Queen appointed Alfred Poet Laureate. At last he had recognition and an income and he and Emily married.

Two years later they rented Farringford House at Freshwater. Here, the supposedly delicate Emily organised the infrastructure of his life. Thomas Carlyle observed that she was "sick without a disorder."

In response to the Crimean War, Alfred composed *The Charge of the Light Brigade,* one thousand copies of which were distributed to the troops at the front. By 1856 they were able to buy Farringford. Emily described it as a "miracle of beauty."

Their first baby died within hours of birth but two sons Hallam and Lionel survived. The great and the good came to visit, Alfred's genius was revered and life seemed complete.

In1886 aged only 32 Lionel Tennyson died en route from India. Once again Alfred's faith faltered. When Emily grew too infirm to act as his bodyguard, it fell to son Hallam to take on the role.

Two of Alfred's closest friends were **W G Ward** of Weston Manor [see Chapter 1] and **Sir John Simeon** owner of both the St John's Estate in Ryde and Swainston Manor at Calbourne. Following Sir John's death in 1870, Tennyson wrote a poem to the *"prince of courtesy"* in the garden at Swainston. The loss hit him hard. Remembering Charles Hallam and his son Lionel, he wrote: *"Three dead men I have loved and thou art last of the three."* An ornate memorial was erected to Sir John at the junction with Carisrooke Road and Castle Road at Newport. *(monument - opposite page, top right Bust Simeon - opposite page, top left, Bust Tennyson - opposite page, bottom)*

To escape the worst of the "tourist season," the Tennysons had a summer residence built at Aldworth and it was there that Alfred died in October 1892, being buried at Westminster Abbey. Emily outlived him by four years and is interred at All Saints Church, Freshwater. (page 44, top) On land donated by the Tennyson family, a new quaint thatched church, names after St Agnes, was built in 1902 at Freshwater Bay.

In 1897, by public subscription, a cross of Cornish granite dedicated to the poet was erected on the highest point of the High Down. The memorial was formally handed over to Trinity House as a beacon to sailors. The ceremony, conducted by the Archbishop of Canterbury, took place on the poet's birthday. *(Page 44 - Tennyson monument - bottom left, memorial palm trees - bottom right)*

History has not always dealt kindly with writers. One such is **Pearl Craigie** (1885-1916), the American novelist and playwright who chose the nom de plume **John Oliver Hobbes**.

Her powerful father and biographer, John Morgan Richards, owner of Steephill Castle at Ventnor, adored her. Pearl's maternal grandfather was a member of the Canadian Parliament and having settled in England, she was presented at court. She was described as serious, strong-minded, and deeply religious.

In February 1887 she married Reginald Walpole Craigie and in July 1890 a son, John, was born but subsequently the marriage failed.

In 1892 to the disapproval of her parents, Pearl joined the Catholic Church. Her first published book was entitled *Some Emotions and a Moral*. Other titles of a serious nature followed.

Most summers were spent on the Island. Among her friends was **Walter Spindler** whose father owned the Old Park at St Lawrence. [See chapter 1]. Walter had work exhibited in Paris and the Royal Academy. In 1895 he did a pen and ink sketch of Pearl and designed the title page for her *Tales of John Oliver Hobbes*. She in turn dedicated her book *A Bundle of Life* to him.

In 1900 Pearl rented St Lawrence Lodge. Walter decorated the place, designed an Italian garden and painted panels in the dining room but she used the house mainly as an office, living with her parents at Steephill Castle. *(above left & right)*

That Pearl was recognised as a writer of substance is underlined by the interest aroused when it was speculated that she would write Disraeli's biography. Her most celebrated novel *Robert Orange* was similar in style to his.

Pearl added a word to the English language – "blimming." Although now out of fashion, it was at the turn of the 20th century a buzz-word, describing a woman who managed to talk endlessly of pleasant things while revealing nothing of herself and hiding the fact that she was cleverer than her husband.

Pearl's view of her sex was not always supportive. She opposed the idea of women jurors as being too emotional stating that Justice was aptly represented by a blindfolded woman, as her sex could not be trusted to see straight!

Pearl made a trip to India in 1902 with Lord and Lady Curzon to attend the famous Durbar. She gave an American lecture tour and in August 1906 was planning a motor trip with her son John. On Sunday morning, having attended Mass at St Wilfred's Ventnor, she left by train for London, telegraphing to say that she had had a good journey. The next morning her parents learned that she had died in her sleep. She was buried at Kensal Green Cemetery and a family memorial is at Ventnor Cemetery. *(above left)*

Her house at St Lawrence, on the corner of Wolverton Road, bears a plaque recording her residence and is now known as Craigie Lodge.

The only son of a minister and schoolmaster, being a frail child, **Henry de Vere Stacpoole** (1863-1951) spent much of his youth in the south of France. For many years writing success eluded him and he worked as a ship's surgeon. There was a sunburst in his early forties when he married Margaret Ann Robson (1907) and a year later had a huge success with his story *The Blue Lagoon* that went into many editions, languages and films. Although remembered as a writer of romantic fiction, under the pseudonym Tyler de

Saix, he wrote darker accounts of the atrocities in the Congo, prompting Sir Arthur Conan Doyle to institute an enquiry. He and Doyle both nursed a belief in fairies, following the fake photographs produced by Cottingly.

Stacpoole founded the Penguin Club dedicated to birds injured by oil pollution. He and Margaret set up home at Cliff Dene at Bonchurch and when she died in 1934 he presented the village pond and a bird sanctuary to the villagers in her memory. *(opposite page, top right)* Three years later he married her sister but both unions were childless.

Stacpoole published more than sixty books set in many locations and reflecting his travels. Living to be eighty-eight, he died at Shanklin hospital and was buried in the new churchyard at Bonchurch. *(opposite page, bottom right, plaque at his home of Cliff Dene)*

Among Stacpoole's friends was the poet **Alfred Noyes** (1880-1958), son of a grocer who moved to Lisle Combe at St Lawrence with his second wife Mary in 1929. *(above left)* With his first wife Kate, daughter of the American consul, he had worked in the States before taking a post with the Foreign Office during the First World War, his sight debarring him from active service. A prolific poet, like Stacpoole, one work eclipsed his others, the poem *The Highwayman*.

During World War Two he and Mary moved to North America, returning to the Island

in 1949. Tragically by this time he had lost his sight. He died at Ryde hospital in 1957 and having converted to Catholicism, is buried in the St Saviour's churchyard at Totland. *(previous page, top right)*

By virtue of her longevity, **Elizabeth Sewell** (1815-1906) overlapped with all the writers featured in this chapter. Elizabeth was 29 when John Sterling died and 70 when Pearl Craigie was born.

Elizabeth was born in Newport one of twelve children. Her father, a solicitor, died in 1842 when £3,000 in debt. From the age of 15 she helped to educate her sisters having in turn attended Miss Crooke's school at Newport. Thus started a lifelong mission to promote moral education for girls, exemplified in her wordy tome *"Principles of Education Drawn from Nature and Revelation and Applied to Female Education in the Upper Classes."* She also wrote popular, moralistic novels for young ladies, her views featuring strongly in her writing. *(above - copyright with Ventnor Heritage Centre)*

In 1849 Elizabeth travelled with the Swinburnes and their twelve-year old son **Algernon** to the Lake District where they met Wordsworth. The Swinburnes were high church and one wonders what Elizabeth later made of Algernon, a *"fragile little creature,"* whose father, an Admiral, abhorred his love of poetry. Algernon's first memory of his

parent was being thrown headfirst into the sea. In later life he denounced Christianity and many of his poems incorporated the experience of being flogged, to which Algernon seems to have been partial. At Oxford he came into contact with the pre-Raphaelites and windows by William Morris and Burne Jones are in St Lawrence church. Alcohol and the unrequited love of his cousin Mary Gordon of Northcourt blighted Algernon's life. He retained a love for his childhood home of East Dene at Bonchurch and was buried in that village. *(above left & right)*

Nothing altered Elizabeth's view of the preordained place of the sexes – *"Boys are sent into the world...to govern and direct...girls are to dwell in quiet homes, to exercise a noiseless influence."* It was her belief that *"obedience is the primary object of all sound education,"* and that *"A woman who is not feminine is a monster in creation."*

Elizabeth did not marry. She donated the St Boniface Diocesan School (Mitchell Avenue) to Ventnor and her wish to die last of her sisters was granted when on August 17 1906 she passed away at her home at Ashcliffe in Bonchurch. She is buried in Bonchurch graveyard. *(2nd row, above left & right)*

When the American poet and playwright **Henry Wadsworth Longfellow** visited the Island in 1868, he was captivated by the beauty of Shanklin Chine with its 45' waterfall

and chalybeate spring. Longfellow, who published more than one hundred poems, wrote a verse entitled *Inscription on the Shanklin Fountain* that was incorporated in his book of verse *In the Harbor*.

A shield bearing the lines features on the brick column from where the adventurous may sample the waters. *(above left & right)*

Sometimes among the native graves a more exotic bloom takes root. In Freshwater churchyard lies **Anna Mae Bosler Ellis** (1858-1911) who, so her epitaph tells us, was for 25 years a musical and dramatic critic, authoress and journalist. Anna Mae was born in Dayton Ohio. By the 1890s, using the pseudonym **Max Eliot** she became a columnist for the Boston Herald producing a regular, cosy feature entitled "Chats about Folk" designed to appeal to American women.

Anna Mae married Granville Alden Ellis, a publisher and at the beginning of the 20th century they lived in London where she continued as American Correspondent for the Herald. As so often happens, how they came to be on the Island is not recorded but on February 20 1911 Anna Mae died at Freshwater. Her loving husband erected a red marble obelisk in her memory. *(opposite page, top left & right)*

Circumstance turned **Professor John Milne** (1850-1913), the son of a Rochdale wool dealer, into the leading expert in the field of seismology.

Following an impressive three years at Kings College London, John specialised in geology at the Royal School of Mines. His career took him to Germany and Canada and in 1875 he was appointed Professor of Geology and Mining at the Imperial College of Engineering, Tokyo.

On February 22nd 1880 Tokyo residents experienced an after shock from the huge earthquake at Yokohama. This led Milne to investigate, uncovering the inadequacies of recording such events. For sixteen years he worked on a design for a successful seismograph.

Six years after his arrival in Japan, he fell in love with Tone, the daughter of Jokei Horikawa, abbot of a Buddhist temple. They married and in 1895, returned to England, buying Shide Hill House on the outskirts of Newport, turning it into a centre for the study of seismology. *(page 52 top)*

John's contribution to science was recognised when he was granted a fellowship of the Royal Society in 1887. He was described as a kind man with a sense of humour and a taste for adventure, having gone to Iceland as a boy without telling his parents. He wrote several books on subjects related to his work.

John died at home on July 31st 1913 and was buried at St Paul's churchyard, Barton, Newport and Tone returned to Japan. In 1974 the Japanese Ambassador planted a flowering cherry, alas now dead, at Shide, in remembrance of the "father of seismology." *(opposite page top left & right)*

Henry Knight (1820-1895), the inventor of the tin opener, was also renowned as a man given to dissension. A *"dealer in marble ornaments,"* he and his wife Harriet came to Ryde in the–mid 19th century where he purchased the trendy Victoria Arcade built to celebrate Queen Victoria's accession. He let out small basement shops to make money.

Inventive by nature, he patented several items although they brought him little reward. His horse clippers were similar to those used in barbers' shops while his automatic weighing machine ended with a legal case. His greatest success was his tin opener patented in 1881 - a short pointed blade, a piece of bent metal resting on the lip of the tin and a handle. It was simple, light and portable. He sold the patent to Crosse and Blackwell and it became a household tool.

In that same year Henry was broke but, undeterred, he joined the local council, a cosy network of men who did not take kindly to his presence. His business continued to do badly and in 1890 he was declared bankrupt.

His sons had taken up photography, no doubt inspired by the success of Henry's one time tenant **Cornelius Jabez Hughes** (1819-1884).

Hughes started his working life as a tailor and ended as a photographer, dying with £10,000 in the bank. In Knight's Victoria Arcade he took over a Mr Lacey's business and his efforts proved to Queen Victoria's liking. Soon he was summoned to Osborne House to photograph the royal family and visiting dignitaries. *"By Appointment to Her Majesty,"* appeared on his work. He built his own premises next door to the arcade at Regina House, an elegant four-storey building. The statues still gracing the roof were no doubt purchased from Knight. *(page 54, top)*

Unlike Knight he eschewed local politics but one blow overshadowed an otherwise successful career. In 1878, Jabez's only son Alfred, also a photographer, died in peculiar circumstances. He was found in St James's Park, London, possibly having taken prussic acid. The details were hushed up but he had been suffering from ill health. He left a wife and three children. When Jabez died he chose to be buried with his son in London. His wife Esther survived him.

Shortly before his death Hughes went into partnership with **Gustav Mullins** from Jersey who worked as his assistant. It was to Mullins that the Royal Warrant *"Photographers*

to Her Majesty at Ryde" was granted. A sociable man, the County Press reports that to celebrate the Queen's Diamond Jubilee, Mullins presented a portrait of Her Majesty to all those present at a dinner for the poor held at the Town Hall, where a toast to him was proposed by the Mayor. Mullins continued to trade under the joint names for thirty years but gradually business slumped. Photography became widely accessible and in 1910 he was declared bankrupt. He died in December 1921 aged 67 and is buried in Ryde cemetery.

While Hughes and Mullins were achieving photographic success in Ryde, at the other end of the Island a bored housewife was experimenting with the camera presented to her by her daughter. **Julia Margaret Cameron** (1815-1879) had moved to Freshwater to be near her friends the Tennysons, buying some fishermen's cottages and knocking them into an impressive house with sea views which she named Dimbola, after her husband's tea plantations in Ceylon. The new hobby became an obsession.

When Tennyson embarked on writing *Idylls of the King,* she illustrated the work. His presence in Freshwater saw a stream of influential visitors and soon Cameron was capturing their portraits for posterity. To her belong images of Darwin, Herschel and of course, Tennyson himself. Her niece Virginia Wolf was sufficiently amused to write a play about the goings on at *Freshwater* while a scandal titillated the visitors when the painter

George Frederick Watts married that slip of a girl, Ellen Terry.

Julia entered various competitions but as a woman and an amateur, her efforts were viewed with some disdain. She was however extremely knowledgeable about the chemistry involved and her work is now revered as among the great portraiture of the 19th century. *(above left)*

The Call of the East saw Julia and Charles return to Ceylon complete with their coffins and there they died.

Regina House once occupied by Hughes and Mullins is at the time of writing a computer shop, while Julia Margaret Cameron's home at Freshwater Bay is a museum dedicated to her art.

Two young American icons, victims of their own fame, are recognisable by their surnames alone. The charismatic **Jimi Hendrix** cast in bronze by John Swindells stands in Mrs Cameron's garden at Dimbola, facing Afton Down where he performed days before his death. With an eye for both genius and beauty she would no doubt be delighted. *(previous page, 2nd row, left & right)*

At Shanklin, the Isle of Wight Rock and Roll Society placed their own tribute in Rylstone Gardens, a plaque recording the life of **Elvis Presley** *"His Memory Lives On." (previous page top right)*

Four
The Sea Shall Have Them

"Here lies One Whose Name is writ in Water"

Epitaph of John Keats.

Between Christmas 1889 and Burns Night 1890, the *Irex,* en route from Glasgow to Rio carrying a consignment of iron pipes, encountered non-stop storms. A sailing ship with a steel hull, it was her one and only voyage. On board was a crew of thirty-four and two stowaways.

Already two seamen had suffered injury. Thirty-seven-year old **Richard Sterne** sustained a broken arm and leg when the cargo shifted. The captain, James Hutton ignored pleas to put him ashore, but cruelly buffeted in the Bay of Biscay, they finally turned back. The captain had hardly slept since leaving Glasgow and in darkness the ship met with the ominous outline of the Needles. Helpless, the Irex was driven onto the rocky shore of Scratchell's Bay.

The first victims were the captain, the mate and the boatswain, swept away on a huge wave as they tried to lower a boat - a useless endeavour as it had no bung. In terrible weather the crewmembers clung to the rigging. Three were battered away, crushed by the cargo or swallowed by the angry sea. One, the oldest, was simply known as Old Harry.

It was not until daylight that their plight was discovered but attempts to reach them failed. The captain of the *Hampshire,* a steamship sheltering off Totland Pier, volunteered to tow the lifeboat through the Needles but even in Scratchell's Bay itself, the lifeboat failed to battle against the waves.

The next plan was to fire a line aboard the stricken ship and bring the men ashore by breeches buoy. The distance was some 400 feet in a raging sea and already it was almost dark. A first crewman took the plunge and to the joy of everyone safely reached the cliff top. Next was Richard Sterne. With two broken limbs one can imagine his agony.

A detachment of soldiers from Golden Hill Fort arrived to help and throughout the

night men were inched to safety. The last, a young lad secured by a blanket to the rigging, was rescued the following day.

The plight of the *Irex* became a cause celebre. The heroic coastguards and soldiers were received by Queen Victoria, then on her Christmas visit to Osborne, while her daughter Princess Beatrice visited the sick and injured housed in the Needles Fort. At the same time controversy raged over the conduct of the Totland lifeboat crew. The boatmen themselves were divided as to whether they could have done more.

There was one more fatality. The badly injured Richard Sterne died a week after the rescue. His wife was brought from Greenock to be with him and his last words were in praise of the kindness he had received. Along with the others he was buried at All Saints Church, Freshwater where the Queen herself erected a headstone. *(Irex Cottages are in Clayton Road Freshwater - top left & right)*

Many seamen owe their lives to **John Dennett** of Clatterford the man credited with the success of the breeches buoy. Various innovations had been tried but it was John's rocket that enabled the equipment to be successfully fired from shore to ship as evinced by the rescue of the *Irex* above.

6
William McNeile
Captain - " Lotus "
Wrecked 19 Oct 1862
11 Drowned

The first major success was the rescue of the crew of HMS *Bainbridge* off Atherfield when nineteen men were safely brought ashore. Thereafter John and his son, aptly named Horatio, set up in business, producing kits from a workshop in Gunville. John died in 1852 but his rockets continued to see service.

Both John and Horatio are buried in St Mary's Carisbrooke behind railings, near to a fine old yew tree. *(above left)*

Sometimes one life affects another in unforeseen ways. When Jabez Balfour [see chapter 6] built the grandiose Royal Spithead Hotel at Bembridge he could not know that it would result in the drowning of a nine year old girl on Boxing day, 1907. **Elaine Rivis Anderson** (1898 – 1907) was spending Christmas with her Aunt Jessie Hawkes who ran the hotel. Elaine's parents lived in Aldershot and she was no doubt company for Jessie's daughters, Kathleen and Mabella. On Boxing Day, Elaine and Mabella went outside to play. One of the features of the hotel was its proximity to the harbour and the girls gravitated to the sea wall. The wind being strong, Mabella returned home with her hoop, expecting Elaine to follow but she was never to see her cousin again.

It does not take much imagination to see the busy aunt asking after her niece. She sent first Mabella, then Kathleen to call her for lunch but they could not find her. Perhaps annoyed that she had to stop what she was doing, Jessie, along with her son Neville, went to look for her. Annoyance quickly turned to anxiety. Before long everyone in the village was looking for Elaine but by dark, she had not been found.

It was not until eleven o'clock the next morning that her body was discovered on the shore. An inquest concluded that her death was accidental and Elaine was buried with her grandmother Jane Anderson at St Luke's Chapel, Lanes End, Bembridge.

Nearly a hundred years later, Rob Jennings, on holiday on the Island, was sufficiently moved by this tragedy to unearth the story *(see acknowledgements)*.

Poor Jessie suffered another tragedy when her only son **(George) Neville Forde Hawkes**, a trooper in the Royal Horse Guards, died at Ypres. He was twenty.

The Royal Spithead Hotel was demolished in 1989 to make way for a town house development called Solent Landing.

With more than sixty miles of coastline and treacherous currents, drowning is an all too familiar part of Island life.

In 1837 the Lymington to Yarmouth mail wherry with twelve people aboard ran into trouble and capsized. Ten were drowned. On April 6th three of the passengers, **James and Ellen Brian and Ellen Murphy** were laid to rest in Yarmouth graveyard.

Similarly a boat ferrying men of the Royal Artillery Ist Battalion North Ireland Division across the Solent to Yarmouth on November 18th 1898 sank and seven were lost. Their comrades erected a headstone in their memory in Yarmouth cemetery. A few weeks later, **Gunner Solomon Grimeson** was discovered washed up on the beach at Cliff End and his name added to the death toll.

October is *the* month for hurricanes. On Sunday 18th October 1862 as a storm brewed and the coastguard stood by, a ship, the *Ellen Horsfall,* was driven into Grange Chine. Thanks to the bravery of an unnamed seaman everyone was brought to safety. Unknown to them however, another ship had run aground at Whale Chine. This crew was not so lucky. The barque **Lotus** out of Greenock and carrying fourteen people was headed for London. Travelling from Demarera with a cargo of rum and sugar her end was swift, breaking up before a rescue could be attempted. Only two men survived. Thereafter the Press conducted an inquest of huge proportions.

The Lotus was old and probably un-seaworthy. The other hazard was in her cargo of rum.

Crowds of locals were soon on the scene, making away with casks and ship's timbers and accusations began flying as to whether the lure of the rum had taken priority over any rescue attempt. Drunkenness at the scene was reported and feelings ran high.

Whatever the truth, **Captain William McNeile** of Androssen and his mainly Scottish crew died. They are buried in Chale churchyard. *(page 59, above right)*

Sunday March 24th 1878 and Ventnor seafront was lively with promenaders, welcoming a bright, if sharp, spring sunshine. Some stopped to look out to sea where a ship in full sail was scudding along at speed. There was a moment of nostalgia, for steamships were fast making inroads.

Too quickly the sky darkened, the wind strengthened and the spring scene was obscured by an angry flurry of snow. The walkers fled for shelter. When they emerged, the sailing ship had gone.

HMS Eurydice, named for the nymph beloved of Orpheus, was nearly home. En route from Bermuda to Dunkirk she would pass near John White's shipyard at Cowes where she had been fitted out as a naval training ship, still reliant solely on sail. On board were more than three hundred sailors, mostly cadets. Within minutes on that fateful Sunday she was transformed from a vessel in full sail to an assortment of spars and flotsam, drifting in the squally wind.

Another ship, the Emma, coming upon this disaster searched desperately for survivors. Of those picked up, only two lived. Many of the crew had been below decks and simply gone down with their ship.

As with the sinking of the Irex, Queen Victoria, resident at Osborne, sent a telegram of condolence. This sudden tragedy shocked the Island - so many young lives.

There was a court martial but the findings were never satisfactorily explained. Why had the ship sunk so quickly? Why was she in full sail when the weather was worsening? Was there sufficient ballast to keep her steady? Were her gun ports open so that water rushed in?

A salvage operation was organised. The first step was to float Eurydice into shallow water to remove the bodies. Two hundred coffins were shipped in for the purpose and this was finally achieved in Sandown Bay. Despite the awful stench of rotting corpses, the beaches were crowded with sightseers. To add to the difficulties the royal yacht Osborne brought the Prince of Wales and family to view the proceedings. Those who went on board the wreck were sick for days afterwards.

Many of the cadets had simply been washed out to sea. The majority of those recovered were buried on the mainland but seven unidentified men were laid to rest in Shanklin Cemetery and seven more in Christchurch graveyard at Sandown where monuments were erected. *(next page, top)*

In one of those ironic kick the cat responses, blame was heaped on the captain of the Emma which, being a temperance ship carried no liquor. It was argued that had she done so, some of those picked up might have been revived by a shot of brandy.

On March 10 1888, the **S V Sirenia**, returning from San Francisco en route to Dunkirk stumbled into thick fog and rough weather, running aground off Atherfield Ledge. On board were Captain McIntyre, his family and twenty-seven crewmembers. In spite of the terrible sea conditions the Brighstone lifeboat *Worcester Cadet* managed to take off the captain's family, a female servant and an apprentice. Mrs McIntyre was hysterical with fear, the children being tossed around like dolls, in danger of being washed overboard. One was a baby.

Moses Munt, coxswain of the lifeboat decided not to take on more people but headed for shore, landing his passengers safely.

As the Sirenia was in no danger of breaking up the lifeboat men waited until the following day to attempt a further rescue. By Saturday however conditions were at least as bad. Undaunted, Moses and his crew went out and took off thirteen of the crew. Then, tragedy struck. In the heavy sea the lifeboat capsized, the oars were lost, everyone was flung into the water and Moses Munt, Thomas Cotton the second coxswain and two members of the Sirenia's crew were drowned. With unbelievable courage, some of those who had already twice been to the wreck agreed to make a third journey. Along with local volunteers they succeeded in bringing the rest of the Sirenia's crew ashore.

During the night another disaster had occurred when the Brook lifeboat *William*

Slaney went to the aid of the Sirenia. The assistant coxswain, **Reuben Cooper** was swept overboard and drowned.

The following week the County Press announced that the three men *"fell gloriously,"* and devoted pages to the tragedy.

All the lifeboat men were Islanders born and bred. Along with farm work, the sea was their living – and their deaths. Moses Munt was 58, the father of six children. Thomas Cotton a fisherman was 48 and unmarried, living at Yafford. Rueben Cooper was a bachelor, living at Brook Green with two brothers and a sister.

The funeral took place at Brighstone on the following Wednesday. The muffled church bell tolled as the coffins were taken to the overcrowded church. There was a fourth coffin, covered in floral tributes, containing 24 year old **Leonard Dozler**, one of the Sirenia's crewmembers who had also drowned. With no relatives nearby to mourn him he was taken to the hearts of the villagers.

To mark the tragedy, M C Gillington wrote a poem, *Atherfield Point, March 10th 1888,* which was printed in the County Press.

...Oh roaring sea, oh raging wind,
A seething surf and spray,
Waves thundering black and rattling back
Round maddened bight and bay...

Headstones were erected to the lifeboat men in Brighstone churchyard and a plaque in Brook church records Rueben Cooper's part in the heroic tragedy. *(next page, top right)*

For much of the twentieth century, the name of **Uffa Fox** (1898-1972) was synonymous with yachting on both sides of the Atlantic. Fox's father was a carpenter working on the construction of Osborne House while his mother was housekeeper on the estate. He attended Prince Albert's Whippingham School then took an apprenticeship at S E Saunders in East Cowes launching his career as a designer of planing dinghies, famous for their speed and winning him innumerable races. During the war his design for an airborne lifeboat was widely used in air-sea rescue.

The yachting fraternity was largely aristocratic and because of his modest beginnings, Uffa had to work hard for recognition but in 1952 he was awarded membership of the Royal Institution of Naval Architects. Three times married, jovial, unpredictable, abrasive, ebullient, hospitable, were adjectives used to describe his larger than life character.

Uffa died on October 26 1972 in Worcestershire. A simple granite slab records his life in the churchyard at St Mildred's Whippingham. *(next page, top left)*

On October 28 1887, Edwin Grey, a Ventnor fisherman was out in his boat when he encountered the lugger **Pride of the Sea**. Recognising the skipper **John Moss** as someone who regularly worked the Island waters, he stopped for a chat. Two days later, Grey was giving evidence at the inquest of Moss and his crew.

Sometime on the Sunday morning during a gale, the ship was lost off Yellow Ledge at Luccombe. The Pride of the Sea was a family run boat, co-owned by John Moss and his brother William, regularly working its way from Walmer in Kent to Dorset. Also on board were John's nephew, Charles and two crewmembers, Charles Selth and Henry Kirkaldie.

The first anybody knew of the tragedy was when John's body was washed up in Sandown Bay. Aged 53, he left behind a wife and six children. William was married but had no family while Charles was single. Henry Kirkaldie aged 34 was the sole support of his mother, while Charles Selth left behind a wife and daughter. They were all experienced seamen. The day before, a sixth crewmember called Adams had been on board but fate had intervened and he had been transferred to another vessel as pilot.

Friends and fellow seamen erected a monument to their memory at Shanklin cemetery, bearing the words of the hymn Eternal Father and also observing, ominously that *"the son of man cometh at an hour when ye think not"* (St Luke). A verdict of accidental drowning due to a storm was recorded. *(Fastnet memorial - 2nd row, above right)*

In 1924 a yachtsman, Weston Martyr, was so inspired by a Bermuda yacht race that he suggested that something similar should be undertaken around British shores. The result was the **Fastnet Race**, over 608 miles of demanding seamanship starting from Cowes, rounding the Fastnet Rock and returning to Plymouth. The first race attracted seven yachts, not all of them completing the course. The challenge grew in popularity and in 1957 the Admiral's Cup was introduced making this the most hotly contested event in the world.

In 1979, 303 ships set off from Cowes, facing a vicious storm during which nineteen men lost their lives.

Walk into the Holy Trinity Parish Church in Cowes and its link with the sea is obvious. The walls are lined with plaques to members of the Royal Yacht Squadron. Following an appeal by the Royal Ocean Racing Club, a memorial terrace garden to those who lost their lives in that disastrous race was created in the graveyard. The memorial features blocks of stone imported from the Fastnet Rock. The dedication took place on the tenth anniversary of the tragedy. *(above left & right)*

Within eighteen months, the Cox family of Freshwater suffered a double tragedy of cruel proportions. On November 20th 1932, twenty-two year old **David Horace Cox** and his twenty year old friend **William Patrick Hope Pollock** were sailing a hired boat from

Newtown to Yarmouth when it capsized. It was discovered off Ryde. Neither young man was found.

Whatever **Robin Murray Cox** felt about his brother's death it did not deter him from planning a boating holiday in the summer of 1934. To this end he hired a yacht the *Hobo* intending to sail from Burnham-in-Crouch to Newtown ready for the vacation. When it did not reach the planned stop at Dover, the alarm was raised. The family clung to the hope that their boy might have been picked up but that was not to be.

To mark the loss, a stone cross stands on the beach off Hampstead Ledge well maintained although largely obscured by greenery. It carries the fatalistic acknowledgement that *"The Sea is His."* *(previous page, top right) (general burials over 100 years at Chale - previous page 2nd row, bottom)*

Five
For God and Empire

"And priests in black gowns were
walking their rounds
And binding with briars my joys
and desires."

William Blake

In 1804, the first non-conformist minister arrived to take up his post on the Island to be greeted by a congregation of eight. In his youth **Daniel Tyerman** (1773-1828) had been a bit of a lad but everything changed when in 1793 a disturbing dream warned him not to accompany his friends on a trip along the Thames. When he heard that their boat had capsized drowning them all, he turned to the church being ordained as a Congregationalist minister.

Daniel threw himself into his ministry, helping to organise Newport's Reading Room and as secretary of the Isle of Wight Bible Society. In seventeen years he built up a vibrant congregation but the wider world called. In 1821 he was selected for an ambitious mission to visit the Pacific, Asia, Australia, Africa and America to report on the progress of the London Missionary Society.

In May, he and George Bennett of Sheffield set out aboard a whaler, heading for a vast scatter of Polynesian islands. They faced the vagaries of the weather, disease, the hostility of local communities plus the disgust of visiting whalers who resented the prudish behaviour imposed upon the converted Polynesians.

There was some success in the Pacific but in other areas the intrepid duo was lucky to escape with their lives. Christianity made little impact on either the convicts or the Aboriginal peoples of Australia and even less on the Hindu culture of India. By the time they reached Java they had been away for four years.

In 1827, en route to Madagascar the two men reached Mauritius. They faced a delay of 6 months because the climate of Madagascar was considered too hostile. Hearing

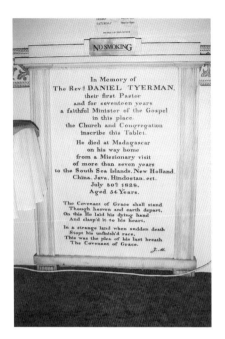

that the prospect of conversion was good they waited but hurricanes and humidity began to take their toll. Finally they made the four-day voyage on a bullock boat and began a gruelling journey inland. Tyerman recorded that: *"...the journey is appalling, and no description can give an adequate idea of it."* Shortly afterwards he fell ill. In an effort to help him, Bennett bled him, probably putting the last nail in his coffin.

The pair had been away from England for seven years and two months.

Tyerman, described as short and stocky with thick curly hair, had before his epic journey twice married and had three sons and two daughters. Bennett, despite a horrific sea voyage, survived the journey home arriving in England in June 1829.

On the Island Tyerman's congregation erected a tablet to record his heroic journey standing in what is currently Beavis's china shop on the corner of Node Hill. *(above left)*

When it comes to being Good, one can't help feeling that St Peter would certainly admit **Francis and Harriette McDougall**. Francis trained as a surgeon then took holy orders and in June 1847 was appointed as missionary to modern day Borneo.

The region was ruled by an extraordinary Englishman, James Brooke, who was the model for Joseph Conrad's Lord Jim. Brooke adopted the title of Rajah and donated land for a mission, encouraging the Christianisation of the local Malays, Dyaks and Chinese. It took Francis, Harriette and their son a year to reach Kuching. On arrival it was left to them to build a church, a house, run a dispensary, erect a school, negotiate their way around the inter-tribal conflicts, cater for the entire mission – and of course convert the locals. Francis held services in three different languages.

In 1855 he was consecrated Bishop of Labuan and Sarawak. Two years later a Chinese insurrection threatened their lives. Harriette was invited to a victory celebration at which the heads of defeated tribesmen were served up. As she stoically reported: *"this was my first and last visit to a Dyak feast."*

During their mission to bring Christianity to Borneo the McDougalls saw their four children die but their faith seems to have remained unshaken.

When Francis died in 1886 he had served as Vicar of Shorwell, Rector of Mottistone, Archdeacon of the Isle of Wight and Canon of Winchester where he is buried. A monument in red marble commemorates their lives in Shorwell churchyard.

In a bizarre reversal of fortunes, in 2005 the church in Borneo considered sending missionaries to Britain. *(opposite page, top right)*

If the **Reverend Legh Richmond** (1772-1827) has left a legacy to the Island it is in immortalising two young women who would otherwise have long been forgotten.

Richmond came from Liverpool where his father was a physician. His early interest was in music but it was to the church that he congregated, and having been ordained in 1797 he moved to the Island as curate of Brading and Yaverland.

Richmond's religious views were of a strongly evangelising nature and during his eight years at Brading he accumulated material for the book that was still published nearly a century later. Under the collective title *Annals of the Poor* Richmond recounts spiritually uplifting tales of ordinary folk who found their way to heaven.

Elizabeth Wallbridge, the Dairyman's Daughter saved her family's souls before herself succumbing to illness. The real Elizabeth lived at Arreton, her cottage is still there and her recently replaced headstone can be seen in the churchyard.

The Young Cottager recounts the life of **Jane Squib**, a member of Richmond's Saturday School. Legh ominously reminded the children that they were not too young to die. On "mild and quiet" little Jane this had a profound effect. During a long illness she prepared herself for heaven and because of her innate goodness, Richmond admitted that his pupil became his teacher. Jane is buried in Brading churchyard and her cottage still exists in the Mall. *(next page, top)*

A third subject *The Negro Servant* is remembered only by his slave name – **William**.

This *"very young-looking man, with a sensible, lively and pleasing countenance,"* declared himself glad to be enslaved, being brought from the darkness of Africa into the light of America where he found Jesus – a sentiment difficult to share! William is welcomed by poor, Christian souls in the village and baptised, thereafter being carried off by his master. Let us hope, in spite of the circumstances, he had a fulfilling life.

Leaving the Island Legh eventually became rector of Turvey in Bedfordshire devoting himself to promoting the British and Foreign Bible Society, the Church Missionary Society and the Society for Promoting Christianity among the Jews.

He found a supporter in the Duke of Kent, father of Queen Victoria, becoming his chaplain. Legh's missionary work extended as far as Scotland. The death of two sons in short succession affected his health. He died on May 8th 1827 at Turvey, probably from the consumption that struck down the young women of his earlier stories.

While men like Francis MacDougall and Daniel Tyerman devoted their lives to service abroad, others confined themselves to their native shores.

On December 1 1892 **Charles William Smith** (1817-1892) died suddenly at his home at Blackgang. After a lifetime's service to a financial house in London, Charles, a widower retired to the Isle of Wight to marry local spinster Edith Reade, immediately immersing

himself in the work of her family's Christian Mission. It was a marriage made in heaven albeit lasting less than three years.

Charles's claim to fame was as co-founder of the Young Men's Christian Association in 1844. Together with several others, a plan to provide mutual support, accommodation, spiritual succour and education was thrashed out. It was Charles who suggested the name. By 1851 there were branches as far afield as France, India and North America.

Although frail, as the County Press of December 10 1892 reported, Charles's departure was unexpected. Having opened his morning mail, he was waiting for family prayers when: *"in an instant he was absent from the body [and] present with the Lord."*

Carried to the Mission Hall by twelve members of his bible class, a sermon was conducted by Captain Mitchell of Portsmouth and there were *"earnest words of exhortation from Mr Scott of Corve Farm, Chale."* Charles's body was then laid to rest in St Andrew's Churchyard.

In a life of impeccable goodness he wrote numerous tracts published under the name of Christopher, such as: *Hints on the Study of Holy Scripture,* also: *Hints on Bee-keeping in Norfolk*. He designed an improved form of beehive and gave lectures on astronomy.

With someone of such obvious saintliness it would be hard to speak ill on his departure. Resting among the village people, no doubt the continuing renown of the YMCA would fill him with righteous pleasure. *(previous page, top left)*

In terms of constant unwavering Christian commitment, men like Christopher Smith and **Albert Midlane** (1825-1909) must have come from similar moulds. Albert was born and died on the Island. The youngest of a large family, his father died before he was born. His mother Frances was a member of the Congregational church but Albert joined the Plymouth Brethren. Leaving school he worked first for a printer, then an ironmonger and finally set up in business in his own right as tinsmith and ironmonger at 29 Lower St James Street Newport.

From childhood he had a passion for composing hymns, the earliest being published under the name *"Little Albert."* The first appeared in printed form in 1842. His most famous composition was *"There's a friend for Little Children,"* being translated into many languages including Chinese and Japanese. His output was prolific at its height being two hundred pieces a year. He never accepted payment.

Albert wrote regularly to the County Press and for a short period, published his own magazine: *Island Greetings.* In 1851 he married twenty-five year old Maria Granger and they had three children.

By helping a friend he was reduced to bankruptcy but a public fund was set up to rescue him.

Albert died on February 27th 1909 and was buried at Mount Joy Cemetery. A memorial stone was paid for by the Sunday Schoolchildren of Hampshire and the Isle of Wight. His home was at Forest Villa, the Mall, Newport.

Maria survived him by four years. *(previous page, top right)*

One wonders whether Albert and Christopher might have met – and if so, whether they liked each other?

From a distance of 500 years it is hard to grasp the significance of spices to the economy. In the sixteenth century nutmegs, believed to cure everything from the common cold to the plague, were worth more than their weight in gold and the getting of them was hazardous.

The Pope in his wisdom drew an imaginary line from Pole to Pole and presented all trading rights west to the Spaniards and everything east to the Portuguese. He did not allow for the ambition of two Protestant navies – the Dutch and the British.

For centuries Europeans contented themselves with buying spices in Venice. The situation might have continued had not the price soared and the English government made it their business to find their own source. Thus began a frenzied race to locate and secure those dots in the Indian Ocean known collectively as the Spice Islands.

One such voyager was **William Keeling**, put in charge of three ships, the Red Dragon, the Hector and the Consent, the brief being to buy up spices and establish trading posts.

They set sail on April 1 1607. The captain of the Consent went ahead and achieved a singularly successful voyage while Keeling aboard the Red Dragon took a more leisurely approach. Flamboyant, quixotic, he orchestrated performances of Shakespearean plays, his crewmen being occupied in learning their lines and making costumes. The first performance was at Sierra Leone where an audience from the Hector watched a rendering of Hamlet. Continuing his meandering journey, Keeling rehearsed Richard II, laid on fishing competitions and an elephant hunt for the amusement of his men. By the time he arrived in the East Indies, the Consent was already back in England.

At Bantam, the expedition faced a hostile Dutch presence but Keeling succeeded in buying a cargo of spices sufficient to fill the Red Dragon. Sending her home, he transferred his belongings to the Hector and continued to the Banda Islands. Again the Dutch would not permit the Hector to trade but they had pushed the Bandanese too far and in an attack all 42 officers were killed, their heads displayed on lances. Ultimately the Dutch were victorious and Keeling was told to leave. He sailed home having accomplished a successful if erratic mission.

En route he sited the Cocos Islands, named Keeling Islands in his honour. Only two of the twenty-seven are inhabited, now being under the control of Australia.

Keeling, a happily married man, defied company rules by smuggling his wife aboard. Being discovered, she was rowed ashore. The feeling must have been mutual and when William died on the Isle of Wight in 1619 at the age of 42, his *"Sorrowful Wife Anne Keeling"* erected a plaque in Carisbrooke Church, *(page 74)* stating:

> *Fortie and two yeares in this Vessell fraile*
> *On the rough seas of life did Keling saile*
> *A Merchant Fortunate A Captaine boulde*
> *A Courtier gratious yet (Alas) not Old.*
> *Such Wealth, experience, honour and high praise*
> *Few Winne in Twice so manie yeares ordanes.*
> *But What the World Admird, he deemd but drosse*
> *For Christ. Without CHRIST all his gaines but losse.*
> *For him and his deare love, With merry cheere*
> *To the holy Land his last course did steere.*
> *Faith servd for Sailes, the Sacred Word for card*
> *Here was his Anchor Glorie his Reward*
> *And thus With gales of grace, by happie venter,*
> *Through straights of Death heavens harbor he did*
> *ENTER*

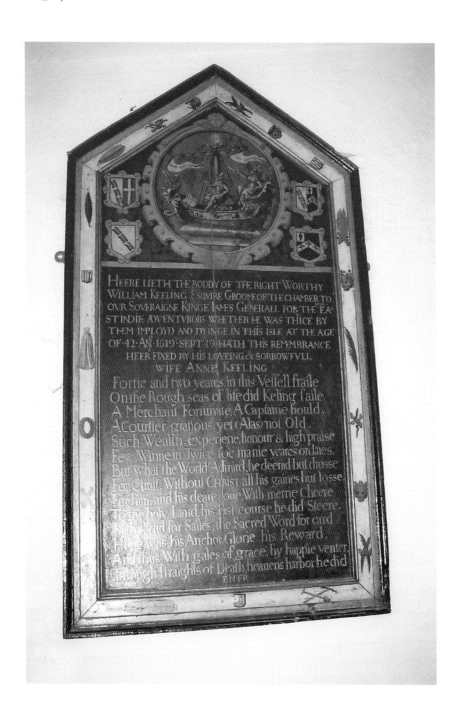

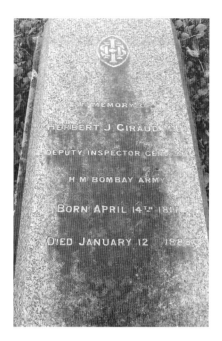 

On the slopes of St Blasius churchyard Shanklin, beneath a red marble slab, are deposited the remains of **Herbert John Giraud** (1817-1888). Herbert's family came to England in 1736 as Protestant refugees but by the time he was born his British roots were well established and he followed his father into the medical profession.

Born in Kent, educated at Edinburgh University, he married Christina Shaw whose father was in the Bombay medical service. The young couple went to India where Herbert excelled first as professor of chemistry and botany, then principal of Grant Medical College and chief medical officer of the delightfully named Sir Jamsetjee Jeejeebhoy's Hospital. He became deputy inspector general of the Bombay army medical service and was called upon to adjudicate in legal cases where medical evidence was crucial.

After a lifetime's devotion he retired to Shanklin living at Heathfield House.

Herbert died on January 12 1888 at the age of 71 having written various papers on chemistry and botany, his best known being *Analysis of the Mineral Springs and Various Well and River Waters in the Bombay Presidency.* Hopefully he rests in peace at the thought of a job well done. *(above left)*

While Herbert Giraud was concerned with medical matters, **Henry Thoby Prinsep** was advising at a high level on finance and administration.

Henry's father John had initiated an interest in India, going there as an army cadet but quickly discovering the gains to be made through trade. Dealing primarily in indigo, he is credited with introducing into Bengal the printing of cotton fabrics. On his return to England he took a seat in Parliament and was appointed alderman of the city of London.

Henry entered the East India College, leaving at the age of 17 to go to Calcutta. Thus began a singularly successful career during which he was appointed Persian Secretary, rubbing shoulders with successive governors-general.

This being a small world, Henry's wife was **Sara Pattle**, the younger sister of the photographer Julia Margaret Cameron [see Chapter 3]. Sara's father had been in the Bengal civil service and produced seven feisty daughters. Sara was important in her own right, initiating what evolved into the Bloomsbury group. On a visit to the Island she met the painter **G F Watts** who being invited to their Holland Park home, *"came to stay three days and stayed thirty years."*

Henry was at Watts' house in Freshwater on February 11 1878 where he died. Along with his wife and his aunt, he is interred in All Saints churchyard. His tombstone tells us that he spent sixty-five years in the service of India. *(previous page, top right)*

One of Prinsep's neighbours in the churchyard is **Selwyn Mitford Palmer** who was head of the Bank of Egypt and financial advisor to the Khedive. Perhaps in death, as in life, they would find plenty to talk about. *(opposite page)*

One can infer a lot from plaques displayed on church walls. Take the **Rushworth** family. In Yarmouth Church a catalogue of their deeds is recorded on marble and a picture of good breeding, advantageous marriage, duty well performed and sacrifice willingly made emerges. That the Rushworths were people who mattered is clear. First to be mentioned is Edward, Island MP, magistrate and recorder who died October 15 1817, aged 62. His wife the Honourable Catherine, was the daughter of Lord Leonard Holmes. They lived at "Farringford Hill," the house that would one day be owned by the Tennysons.

As parents they knew the pain of loss, three children dying in infancy, while in 1812, their son Edward, captain of the *Barbadoes* [sic] died at Port Royal *"a victim of the climate."* He was twenty-five.

After the death of her husband, Catherine lost her fifth son, Henry, a lieutenant on the *Liverpool,* meeting an untimely end at Trincomalee, Ceylon, aged 21. Ten years of quiet grief remained before she joined her family in the hereafter.

Another Rushworth, Rosamond Linda, wife of the Rev Cecil Evan Smith, erected a plaque to the memory of her parents Edward and Adelaide. Edward served as Lieutenant Governor of Jamaica where he died, aged 59. The seafaring tradition continued, cut short when her brother Charles Edward, a midshipman on HMS Agincourt, drowned in 1877 while rescuing a fellow sailor.

As Edward Rushworth was a victim of the tropics, so was **Ewan Robert Law** who died at Shanklin in July 1858. Ewan served aboard HMS Seringapatam, a ship named after the battle of 1799 at which Tipu Sultan of Mysore was defeated. He was struck down by the *"effects of the climate,"* aged 39. His grieving parents buried him in Bonchurch old church.

There seems not to have been the slightest doubt that **Sir Robert Oliver** died in a good cause. A fine stained glass window in the church of St Mary and St Rhadegund at Whitwell, records how he:

> *...in the faithful discharge of his duties*
> *to his sovereign and his country was called to his rest.*
> *He died at Bombay of sunstroke on the 5th August 1848*
> *And was buried in Bombay Cathedral...*

His wife Rachel Mary died at Millfield, Ryde.

A more plaintive plaque adorns the wall of St Michael the Archangel at Shalfleet. On February 7 1829 thirty year old **Thomas Cole**, returning from naval service in the West Indies, perished at sea aboard the HMS Nightingale. His sorrowful only sister records a: *"brave, unassuming, religious, affectionate brother and a dutiful son."*

The Waterworth family of Newport lost several of their nine children in the cause of empire. Thomas of the Royal Navy died at Jamaica aged 24 years, Albert of the "Honourable East India Company marines" died at Deristan in the Persian Gulf aged 18 years and George died at Hondas, aged 20 years. They also lost Edward-Henry a surgeon. A marble plaque records this sad history in St Andrews church, Chale.

At St Helens church tribute is paid to **Emily Heathfield** who, along with her husband, child and nurse, perished at Oude on 3rd June 1857 during the Indian Mutiny. **William Henry Dennie**, aide de camp to Prince Albert, fell on the *"field of victory"* at Jellalebad being buried beneath the fort *"afar from Christian Lands."* His sacrifice is recorded at St Mary's Carisbrooke.

These memorials seem essentially British, understated, stiff upper lip, doing one's duty, and yet one wonders if beneath it all there was ever an unacknowledged faltering, as if in daring to question the purpose of it all it would undermine their very reason for being?

Six
Naughty Naughty

"His mourners will be outcast men,
And outcasts always mourn"

Oscar Wilde

The Church is not always full of saints. One doubtful angel was **Nicholas Udall** from Southampton (1504-1555), minister at All Saints Calbourne.

In 1534 he became headmaster of Eton, a *"poorly paid but honourable post"* – and one that gave considerable scope for whipping small boys. During his headmastership certain items of value were stolen and Udall was charged with "burglary". He also appears to have confessed to committing "buggery," and although the latter was a capital crime, Udall served time in the Marshalsea prison but survived the incident.

In 1534 he produced a Latin primer that was used for fifty years and became an established writer and translator, his career punctuated by lawsuits in which he was both plaintiff and defendant.

His most memorable creation was a play, *Ralph Roister Doister*, to be performed by young boys and recognised as the first comedy in the English language. He wrote pieces for the wedding of Anne Boleyn, had the patronage of Queen Katherine Parr and one of his plays was performed in front of Queen Elizabeth. On the down side, while serving as Canon for St George's Chapel at Windsor he was investigated following a jewel robbery although not charged. He was also sued for taking money to provide a lucrative post as caterer to the army and failing to come up with the goods. Fortunately for him, at that moment he was shipped off for three years to Calbourne. He died two years later.

Lying uncomfortably in his suit of armour, **Sir Edward Horsey** (died 1583) appears to pray for his immortal soul from his marble couch in St Thomas's church, Newport. He may have needed to having been exiled to France following an attempt to overthrow Queen Mary 1. Queen Elizabeth was slow to invite him back but he made himself useful as a spy and all was eventually forgiven. In 1556 he was appointed Captain of the Isle of Wight, then Justice of the Peace for Hampshire and the Island.

While in France, Horsey had taken a Huguenot wife, a detail he overlooked when in the 1570s he set up home with Dowsabelle Mills, a widow who had inherited Hasely Manor at Arreton from her husband George. Mills and his brother John had benefited from the dissolution of Quarr Abbey being paid £1,000 for the construction of Yarmouth Castle and two cow towers at East and West Cowes, using the abbey stone.

Dowsabelle, who seems to have come from "up north," greatly impressed Sir John Oglander with her skills as a hostess. Clearly the irregular alliance did not affect their standing for in 1580 the Portuguese ambassador came to stay. The following year Horsey was struck down with suspected plague, dying in 1583. His fine marble and alabaster tomb bears the family crest. *(above, top right)*

The achievements of **Robert Hooke** (1635-1703) rate with those of Newton and Wren yet he is barely acknowledged in his birthplace of Freshwater. In contrast, during a lifetime spanning much the same period, **Robert Holmes** (1622-92), a bombastic interloper left his mark on the Island in numerous ways.

Holmes was soldier, sailor, explorer and swaggering man of action, whereas Hooke was of poor physique, introspective, a philosopher and academic. Hooke was an Islander while Holmes was disparagingly referred to as an *"Irish livery boy."* Hooke went to

London where he worked on springs, microscopy and rebuilding the city after the Great Fire, his achievements too numerous to list here. Holmes ended his career at Yarmouth as Governor, acquiring huge tracts of land.

Grace Hooke, Robert's niece was born on the Island in 1660. At the age of ten she went to live with her uncle. By the time she was fifteen he confessed to sleeping with her. Thereafter he was beset by jealousy as she attracted various suitors. In 1678 she returned home and word reached him that Holmes was courting her. At about this time Holmes acquired a daughter, Mary. Her mother was never identified but Grace is a likely candidate. Grace's father John, beset by financial worries committed suicide at this time, the anguish of his daughter's pregnancy perhaps pushing him over the edge?

The following year Grace returned to London to keep house for her uncle, remaining with him until she died in 1687, leaving him to mourn.

Eschewing his official residence at Carisbrooke, Holmes built a prestigious house at Yarmouth Castle, currently the George Hotel. He also bought Mary a farm, today's Thorley Manor.

A statue of Holmes in St James's Church, Yarmouth was intended as that of King Louis XIV. When the ship carrying it to France sank, Holmes took the torso and surmounted it with his own head. He died a wealthy man leaving all to his nephew Henry – provided he married Mary. Should he decline, the fortune would pass to his younger brother with the same proviso. Needless to say, Henry agreed and Mary bore him sixteen children. Hooke died alone, bedridden and blind. A chest containing several thousand pounds was found in his rooms. A block of granite outside the Freshwater Co-op at Hooke Hill acknowledges his birthplace. *(opposite page, top left & 2nd row top right)*

Happily the Island is not known as a murder capital but one crime, because of its macabre nature, resonates through the ages. On March 19 1737, **Michael Morey**, a 65 year-old labourer from Arreton was executed at Winchester Gaol for murdering his 14 year-old grandson, James Dove. The horror was perpetuated by the manner of James's death, dismembered and the pieces left in panniers in a wood, to be found only when the maggots had done their work. A motive was never established although there was some suggestion that James's absent father may have left him money.

For a week after James's disappearance, Michal too vanished. When he was taken up he offered no defence but neither did he confess to the murder.

The Moreys occupied a solitary cottage at Sullens in the valley between Burnt House Lane and St George's Down. Several local people were called as witnesses. Michal's son Richard was not sufficiently convinced to disown him, sending food to Winchester Gaol where Michal languished for seven months.

After his execution, Michal's body was returned to the Island and displayed on a gibbet near to the scene of his crime, hanging in chains on a Bronze Age burial mound later named Michal Morey's Hump along from the Hare and Hounds Pub towards the Brading turn-off.

James was buried in Arreton churchyard. Michal, being a felon, was denied a Christian burial and left for the birds to pick.

On December 15 1840, the Baronne de Feucheres died suddenly at her palatial London home. At the news, a sigh of relief wafted across the Channel for although ten years had elapsed since a scandal rocked the French throne, the repercussions were ongoing.

The Baronne's roots were humble. At St Helens, her father Dicky Dawes scraped a living from the seashore, using the proceeds to whet his interminable thirst. He had not married his children's mother and when the cycle of cold and hunger became too great, Jane Calloway sought refuge with her brood in the workhouse.

Her daughter Sophia was kitted out as a maid but ambition drove her to leave the Island. Calling herself **Sophie Dawes**, she found work in a brothel where she met the émigré Duc de Conde. He was in his late fifties, Sophie in her early twenties. It amused him to educate her in the finer points of social life but when the time came to return to France, he did not give Sophie a second thought. Undaunted she followed him and for eighteen months pestered him to take her back. When he succumbed, Sophie had her foot on the ladder of social advancement.

A mistress could not be introduced into French society so Sophie claimed that she was Conde's illegitimate daughter. She then married someone in his service so that she and the Duc could be together. When her new husband realised his mistake, he left her. With nothing to lose, Sophie installed herself as the Duc's mistress.

Sophie then plotted to secure his fortune. In cahoots with Conde's hated relative the Duc d'Orleans, she worked on her lover to leave his estate to Orleans' son. She had already extracted riches for herself but more would come on Conde's death. He resisted persuasion and beatings but Sophie isolated him and in the end he succumbed. That he was weak is certain for even when supporters offered to rid him of his violent mistress he seemed incapable of taking action.

In the meantime, the death of King Charles X of France saw the Duc d'Orleans installed as King Louis Philippe. Sophie now had the access she yearned for to the Court.

Conde had outlived his usefulness. His last desperate plan to escape to Switzerland came to nothing and on the night of August 26/7 1830, he was found hanging from his window frame. In spite of overwhelming evidence to the contrary a verdict of suicide was passed. It was generally believed that he had been strangled.

Although Sophie had money and power, her longed for social position was short lived and Louis Philippe, himself under threat, banished her from the court. In 1837 she sold up her French assets and returned to England.

If Sophie had a saving grace it was family loyalty. Her mother lived with her in France, embracing the religious life and dying in a convent aged ninety. Sophie adopted as her heir her sister Charlotte's daughter. Her other sister Mary Anne married well and in her will, Sophie made a bequest of three million francs to both Mary Anne and their brother James. This familial loyalty was however blackened by one further suspicion. Before returning to England Sophie had quarrelled with her nephew James Dawes. James had been her lackey in France and she secured him the title Baron de Flassans, but over the question of Conde's death he was indiscreet. He succumbed to a sudden, violent illness. His doctor swore it was not the "apoplexy" listed on his death certificate. He was returned to the Island for burial and his aunt erected a tomb bearing the words: *"Erected as a mark of Affection by his aunt, Madame la Baronne de Feucheres."* It was widely believed that Sophie poisoned him.

Sophie herself embraced Catholicism and donated widely to French charities. She died from a heart attack, her death describing how: *"She was stifled quickly, as if strangled by an invisible hand."*

Her burial place is not recorded and her sole memorial is a plaque on the cottage where she was born on the north side of St Helens Green.

In 1848 Louis Philippe of France was forced to abdicate.

Marriage among the gentry was generally rooted in ambition. Title, wealth and land were juggled like balls to the mutual advantage of those concerned. Through a series of opportunistic unions one branch of the Worsley family established itself on the Island gaining the estate of Appuldurcombe at Wroxall. So entrenched were they that two hundred years later the then incumbent, Sir James, confidently ordered that all his belongings should *"go with the possession of and inheritance of Appuldurcombe for ever"* – fateful words, for within a century the house passed out of the family.

The buck stopped with **Sir Richard Worsley** the 7th baronet (1751-1805). Richard spent much of his young life on the Continent, developing an interest in antiquities. When it came to marriage his selected bride was **Seymour Dorothy Fleming**, the youngest daughter of Sir John Fleming of Brompton Park in Middlesex. She had two advantages – she was pretty and she brought with her £70,000. They married on 15th September 1775 and Seymour produced a son and daughter neither of whom survived to inherit the property.

Seymour was hardly the dutiful wife. Glamorous, flirtatious, she openly embarked on a series of affairs. In February 1781 when Richard was Colonel of the Hampshire Militia

he became friendly with **George Maurice Bisset**, an officer in the regiment. After a party at which Richard was absent, Seymour did not return home and Richard discovered that she and George had left together. This public humiliation, the latest in a series of misdemeanours, decided him to sue Bisset for "criminal conversation" with his wife. The upshot was a lurid interest in the case. Bisset claimed that Worsley had actively encouraged the affair and although the judge found for Worsley, the £20,000 damages he hoped for were not forthcoming. He left Court the wealthier by one shilling and to the scorn of society.

That Bisset was a rogue is not disputed. From his home of Knighton Gorges near Newchurch, he ran his own Hellfire Club where Sir Joshua Reynolds, David Garrick and

John Wilkes (who had a house at Sandown), came for entertainment. Prior to the trial, Seymour was a regular visitor. Following the scandal Bisset married the daughter of one of Seymour's lovers and *"grew old and eccentric and syphilitic in his glorious estate."* [Paul Hyland]. His unfortunate heiress elected to marry a clergyman so her dissolute father demolished Knighton Gorges, moving into a gardener's cottage where he died on December 21 1821. Thus vanished one of the most beautiful houses on the Island. *(opposite page, top left)*

Worsley decamped to the Continent for five years. On his return he spent much time at Sea Cottage along the Undercliff with his housekeeper Mrs Smith. Next door at Lisle Combe, his mother watched the classical temples and Greek statues take over.

Ultimately, Seymour didn't do too badly. Reverting to her single name of Fleming, when Sir Richard died she regained her dowry and in the same year married John Lewis Cuchet.

As a breed, the Worsleys had a gift for ostentation. The shell of Appuldurcombe House gives some indication of its grandeur while the Freemantle Gate marking the entranceway from Godshill Park is heroic indeed. *(opposite page, bottom left)* On the Down to the west are the remains of an obelisk erected in 1774 in memory of Sir Richard's ancestor Sir Robert. Once 70' high, it was struck by lightening in 1831 and reduced to a pile of stones. *(opposite page, bottom right - statue ruins)* All Saints church at Godshill abounds with statuary including a hideous sarcophagus weighing 30 tons recalling Sir Richard himself while other Worsleys bask in immortal glory. Similar plaques adorn St George's at Arreton. *(opposite page, top right)*

In happier days Richard had Seymour painted by Joshua Reynolds, sporting a snazzy outfit based on the uniform of the Hampshire Militia. After the "troubles" he refused to pay for the portrait until Sir Joshua gave up and donated it to Seymour's stepfather, Edwin Lascelles.

The line between good and bad is blurred indeed but when it comes to standing in judgement, one trait that is hard to forgive is hypocrisy. Coming from a family steeped in Non Conformist piety, **Jabez Balfour** was thus consigned to the bad – that and the fact that he served 14 years in prison for fraud.

Balfour's mother Clara Lucas was born near Brading. Illegitimate, her father supported her until she was nine and when he died Clara went to London, struggling to survive as a seamstress. This early penury turned her into a devout campaigner for goodness. From her pen flowed such gems as *Moral Heroism and the Trials and Triumphs of the Great and Good,* published in 1848.

Jabez's father Jimmy Balfour was a messenger at the House of Commons and followed his wife rather shakily into the Temperance Movement. Jabez was their youngest child, born in 1843 at a time when they were doing well. He even had the benefit of a

Continental education. Early on Clara recognised his talent although she nursed anxieties as to whether he would employ it to good or bad effect.

Jabez became involved in the Liberator Building Society, intended to free the poor from the yoke of paying rent. This was gratifyingly successful and other schemes succumbed to his Midas touch. He then turned his attention to the Island where there were plans to drain Brading Harbour. It was two hundred years since the last attempt had ended in disaster. The plan was ambitious, to drain the marsh, provide a railway link from St Helens to Bembridge and turn that village into a seaside resort. An embankment was completed by July 1879 and a celebratory cricket match played on the newly reclaimed land but in October the sea swept it all away. Undeterred, Jabez rebuilt the embankment and within six months it was again complete. This time the tide lost and Bembridge grew in popularity, crowned by a railway station and Balfour's splendid Royal Spithead Hotel.

Success favoured his numerous ventures but his empire was built on slippery sand. A downturn in the economy put pressure on his companies' resources and it became clear that his accounting was at the least, imaginative. As his various initiatives came crashing down, he fled to Argentina leaving small investors faced with ruin. For three years Jabez evaded extradition but an enterprising detective succeeded in returning him to London.

Sentenced to gaol, he served part of his sentence at Parkhurst where, in happier times, he had purchased a farm. He catalogued the prison library and was regarded as a model prisoner being released on April 14 1906. His memoirs were serialised in the daily *Dispatch* and, although now in his early seventies, he took work as a mining engineer in Burma.

Returning to England and en route by train to Scotland to take up a new position, he entertained passengers with his adventures. Falling quiet, when they reached their destination they discovered that he had died.

Jabez leaves no statue on the Island but the view across Brading Haven remains a lasting memorial to his time here.

While Jabez was languishing in gaol, a funeral with all the pomp that one could wish for took place at Northwood cemetery. On February 17 1892 shutters were closed, curtains drawn, flags flown at half-mast and the route from Cowes lined with mourners. Floral tributes included violet hearts from the widow and bereaved children. There were wreaths from the Dean of Westminster, Admiral de Horsey, Sir Godfrey Baring, members of the Seely family and Inspector McGlaughlan who kept the crowd in order. Miss Hookey, the dead man's nanny, sent a floral anchor while sixty members of the Court Foresters Isle wore black scarves and carried laurel leaves.

The County Press reported that at the graveside the mourners took one last look *"at the remains of him whom everybody liked."*

The Wards of Northwood House did not like him for a start. Neither would **James Binfield Bird** have wished mourners to dwell on his past association with Jabez Balfour, for he had been involved up to his neck in the scandal that saw Balfour consigned to gaol.

For sixteen years he was Agent to the Ward family but around 1875 unease crept in as to his trustworthiness. The Wards initiated an enquiry and the result was a dispute over the ownership of carriages, horses, and even an iron safe. Mr Bird was asked to vacate the premises.

Fortunately for him, that year the Brading Harbour scheme got under way and he found employment. Later it was to come back to haunt him. When questions were first asked as to the finances of Balfour's empire, Jabez was forced to agree to an enquiry carried out by the respectable London firm of Driver and Co. Their findings confirmed the suspicions, that the corporation's assets were grossly over-valued. Fortunately for Balfour, Mr Driver had in his employ a certain James Binfield Bird who informed his employer that Balfour no longer needed his report. Mr Driver took his fee and thought no more of it.

Bird was now employed to present his own report, his findings being quite the opposite from those of Mr Driver. Balfour assured his creditors that a more capable, straightforward or honest man than Bird did not exist, Bird's version of the situation was accepted and he was awarded a seat on the board of the Lands Allotment Company.

Quite how he avoided being tarnished when the deception was discovered is difficult to believe but Binfield Bird became a pillar of Cowes society, as his obituary shows. Not wishing to speak ill of the dead...! *(previous page)*

Seven
High and Mighty ?

"The rich man in his castle
The poor man at his gate
He made them, high and lowly,
And ordered their estate."

Cecil F Alexander

In their halcyon days, King Charles I and Henrietta Maria produced eight children two of whom were destined to be kings (Charles II and James II) while their daughter Mary was the mother of William of Orange. **Princess Elizabeth** (1635-50) and her brother **Henry** however were condemned to short lives, much of it spent in captivity.

Elizabeth was born at St James's Palace on December 28 1635. When she was seven the country descended into civil war. Fleeing to Oxford, Charles left Elizabeth and Henry in the hands of Parliament who saw them as bargaining tools. They passed through several guardians and were treated to a rigorous religious education. Elizabeth became fluent in Greek, Hebrew, Latin, French and Italian and was regarded as "forlorn," "melancholy" and resigned to her fate.

As the war raged their brother James was brought to live with them. Elizabeth urged him to escape and is credited with helping him to do so, disguised as a woman.

The king's war being lost, in a painful farewell the children were allowed to see him on the eve of his execution. A year later their brother Charles arrived in Scotland ready to claim back the throne. It was decided to move Henry and Elizabeth out of harm's way and, despite the fact that Elizabeth was ill, they were shipped to Carisbrooke where, on September 8 1650 aged 15, she died.

She was buried in a vault in St Thomas's church, Newport, the initials ES carved into the wall. Queen Victoria commissioned a marble statue by the sculptor Marochetti depicting a romantic young heroine, now a focus in the church. A 19th century Post Mortem revealed her to be

crippled by rickets. Two hundred years later Queen Victoria ordered a marble statue by the sculptor Marochetti to depict the young princess's death, now a romantic focus in the church.

Henry went to France and later joined Charles in England but died of smallpox at the age of twenty. *(above)*

Just outside the porch of St George's church Arreton is a brick tomb topped with a stone slab, under which lie the remains of **William Cromwell** (c1667-1729) "grandson" of the Protector. That he is a Cromwell seems certain but exactly who he was is a mystery.

Oliver Cromwell had nine children and some thirty-two grandchildren, none of whom seems to be this particular William.

At first glance the most likely father would be Oliver's eldest surviving son Richard who briefly became Protector on his father's death. In 1649 Richard married Dorothy Maijor of Hursley in Hampshire. Her father acquired land on the Isle of Wight at Horringford where William Cromwell was living. One would assume that he was Richard's child – except that his only son who survived to adulthood, Oliver, died unmarried and childless.

Another of Cromwell's sons, Henry, married Frances Russell of Yaverland and had a son called William – but this William died in 1692. Possibly our William was a great grandson?

The Public Record Office shows that William Cromwell married Martha Cook of Brading who died on February 1742 in her 69th year. Whether or not they produced children is not stated. Hence, we consign William back to the shadowy past. *(opposite page, top left)*

Queen Victoria (1819-1901) had fond memories of Osborne. In 1845 she and **Prince Albert** acquired 1700 acres of East Cowes as a holiday retreat. Albert set about creating a three hundred-room house complete with fire-proof skirtings, central heating and indoor plumbing. Victoria was thrilled with *"dear, modest, unpretentious Osborne."* The prince built Whippingham School for the local children *(top right)* and for his family's spiritual welfare, St Mildred's church, demolishing the earlier Nash design *(bottom left)*. About forty estate cottages followed and a passion for Victorian architecture was unleashed. When Albert died, aged only 42, his sorrowing wife erected a plaque in the royal pew of his church. *(above, right middle)*

Her children all lived to adulthood and with the exception of Louise became parents but theirs was not always a happy lot as depicted in the other plaques in the royal pew.

Her eldest child, **Vicky, the Empress Frederick**, mother of eight children, (including Victoria's favourite the future Kaiser Wilhelm II), lost her baby son **Sigismund** aged two from meningitis, a loss compounded by the death of her favourite boy, **Waldemar**, who succumbed to diptheria in 1879. Both boys are commemorated at St Mildred's and Sigismund's portrait hangs in the nursery at Osborne. *(previous page, bottom right)* In happier times she and her husband Crown Prince Frederick donated stained glass windows to Christchurch Sandown.

Vicky died a few months after her mother of cancer of the spine.

Victoria's second daughter **Alice, Grand Duchess of Hesse** had seven children. Haemophilia claimed her son Freidrich aged only two when he fell from a window and diptheria took her daughter Marie aged four. Alice in turn succumbed to diptheria dying on the 17th anniversary of Prince Albert's death, December 14 1878. Her plaque too is at St Mildred's. *(above)*

Alice's daughter **Victoria**, mother of **Lord Louis Mountbatten** is buried in Whippingham churchyard. *(opposite page, top left)* The bust of Lord Louis himself, who became Island Governor perches on a plinth in St James's square Newport. *(opposite page, top right)*

Haemophilia also claimed the queen's youngest son **Leopold, Duke of Albany** who died after a fall in 1884 aged 31. He is commemorated in the church.

Pity Victoria's youngest daughter **Beatrice**, condemned to be her widowed mother's companion. With rare determination she overcame queenly opposition and married **Prince Henry of Battenberg** but the aching boredom of life with his mother-in-law drove him to fight in the Ashanti war where he died of malaria aged 38. Shipped home, he was buried in a sarcophagus in St Mildred's, joined 46 years later by his wife. Did she suspect that Henry and her wilful, attractive sister Louise might have been lovers? On his death Louise sculpted a strangely erotic image of the dead prince being taken to heaven by an angel. It stands in the Battenberg Chapel. *(page 94, top left)*

Beatrice the widow devoted her life to her role as Island Governor. In 1919 she unveiled the Whippingham war memorial, the first name being that of her son **Prince Maurice** who died at Ypres.

Queen Victoria herself has many memorials. Her statue designed by Percy Stone dominates St James's Square Newport *(page 94, top right)*, while to mark her Golden Jubilee a clock tower designed by Mr R Braxton Peress ARIBA was added to Nash's Institute and a drinking fountain installed in Wootton High Street. The diamond jubilee

was commemorated by a clock tower on Shanklin seafront *(opposite page)* all recording her long association with the Island.

Few roles in Queen Victoria's household could have been less enviable than that of Private Secretary. The post required an ability to marry seemingly impossible differences of opinion held by the most powerful in the land – the Prime Minister, visiting diplomats, the royal children and of course, the queen herself. This Herculean task fell to **Sir Henry Ponsonby** (1825-95) on April 8th 1870.

Ponsonby had a distinguished army career serving in the Crimea. He was then appointed equerry to Prince Albert until the consort's death. His appointment as the Queen's secretary was not popular, as he was a known army reformer with liberal sympathies, both anathema to Victoria. All his skills were called for during the premiership of Gladstone whom Victoria abhorred.

The Queen was often seen as her own worst enemy, hiding away from the public and succumbing to the questionable charms of first John Brown and then Abdul Karim. In both situations, the royal children called upon Ponsonby to make their mother see sense, being too frightened to risk her wrath themselves.

On April 30th 1861, Ponsonby married Mary Elizabeth Bulteel, one of the Queen's maids of honour. It was a love match and the couple produced five children. Mary was

passionate about women's education and was instrumental in the foundation of Girton College. As with those of her husband, her views did not meet royal favour.

When staying on the Island, the family occupied Osborne Cottage and it was here on January 6 1895 that Henry suffered a stroke. In November he died and was buried at Whippingham church. Victoria's son Arthur, Duke of Connaught represented her at the funeral.

Mary Pononsby lived for a further twenty years. Her own liberal views rubbed off on her children to the extent that her son Arthur became a Labour MP – whatever would the queen have thought!

A plaque at Whippingham acknowledges Ponsonby's selfless service.

In Chale churchyard, protected from the great unwashed by iron railings, lie the remains of **Lady Elizabeth Henrietta Cole** (died 1857). Her mother, Lady Elizabeth, eldest daughter of James the 6th Duke of Hamilton, married Edward Smith Stanley the 12th Earl of Derby in 1774. By the time her third child Elizabeth was born, she was more interested in the charms of the rakish John Frederick Sackville, 3rd Duke of Dorset and it was with him that she eloped. It was widely believed that young Elizabeth was Dorset's offspring but Derby ignored the speculation and raised her as his own. With such a shadow hanging over her it is difficult to believe that her childhood was happy. *(above)*

Here under lyeth the body of S[r] William Stephens K[t] some years Lieu[t] Gover[nr] of this Island who dyed 5[br] 26 1697 in the 57th year of his age.

On one side of him lie the remains of Dame Elizabeth his wife who dyed Ian[r]2.94.

On the other his brother Henry who dyed Iun[e] 28.1689.

Also near them lie the ashes of H[is] Mary

Although Derby soon found consolation with a beautiful actress, Elizabeth Farren, he refused to divorce the first Elizabeth or allow her to see her children. His own claim to immortality is as the man after whom the classic horse race was named, decided on the toss of a coin.

Young Elizabeth was "married off" to Stephen Thomas Cole on January 15 1791. Little is known of him other than that he died in 1835. Let us hope that she enjoyed her stay on the Island and that somewhere along the line she found happiness. *(top page 96)*

Clinging on to immortality in the form of a plaque in St Mary's Church Carisbrooke, **Sir William Stephens** (c1650-97) was the first Lieutenant Governor of the Isle of Wight.

The family's Island connection seems to have started in 1588 when Richard Stephens of Christchurch married Elizabeth Dolman of Whippingham, producing four sons.

Our Sir William's father, also William, was an ambitious man. Securing the position of Recorder for Newport when the Parliamentarians came to power he swiftly changed allegiance and was advanced to the position of Steward and Bailiff of the Wight. When the Royalist Lucius Carey lost his seat in Parliament, William was quick to step into his shoes. He bought up numerous Island properties including the manor of Bowcombe conveniently on the doorstep of Carisbrooke Castle. He died in 1659.

Our William, the eldest son, was not driven by the same ambition. He married Elizabeth Hillery, daughter of a Dorset grazier, and although she came with a dowry of £3,000, her wealth and rank were a disappointment to her ambitious in-laws. To appease them William took a captain's commission in the militia and was promoted to colonel by Sir Robert Holmes.

Representing the Island in Parliament but with a sizeable estate to run, William resented the demands on his time. When Homes offered him a post as his deputy, he refused but he could not turn down the King's Commission making him the first Lieutenant Governor of the Island. This demanded the very commitment he was anxious to avoid and Lord Cutts, the next governor, declined to renew his appointment, saying the post required someone having *"no other business to mind."*

Whether from exhaustion, disease or disappointment, William died at the age of 47. His epitaph includes his wife Elizabeth, his brother Henry and three daughters who died in infancy.

His successor, also William, made a marriage that was not approved of – by the bride's family. She may have wished she had listened to them for her epitaph in St Mary's speaks of her many trials and afflictions. In part this was due to the burden of providing for nine children plus entertaining the many hangers-on who visited the house fancifully called *"Buen Retiro"*, built by William at Cowes. In entering Parliament and remembering his father's exhortation to stay out of civic life, William admitted that *"I have done ill in disobeying my father's injunction."* In this he was right. After many years of service he was discarded as the MP and forced to sell the Island properties. His last years were spent in poverty on the mainland, his heir recouping what he could and settling for a life in holy orders. *(previous page)*

Eight
Miscellany

"Life is a jest, and all things show it, I thought so once and now I know it."

John Gay

Somewhere along the timeline that signals the agricultural revolution sits Arreton farmer **James Ruffin Blake** (1833-1900). A man wedded to tradition, James represented the new order, cautiously testing the mechanical innovations and venturing to the mainland for holidays and business trips.

As Queen Victoria's parents were first cousins, so were James's. As she married her first cousin, so did James. His wife was Frances Roach and perhaps because of this consanguinity her first eight pregnancies resulted in miscarriage. Eventually they were rewarded with two children.

The Blakes owned Birchmore and Stone Farms near Newport and almost by right James fell into parish work, being churchwarden for Arreton while giving land for the construction of a Methodist chapel at Blackwater.

He served on virtually every committee, overseeing an ambitious road improvements scheme for which he donated land. Inspector of the workhouse, school secretary (where he visited twice weekly), he administered charities providing food and education for the poor, all of course in addition to running a farm of some 500 acres. In politics he was an active Liberal Party agent.

Frances died in 1895 and in 1900 James sought relief from his ills by visiting the spas at Buxton where he died on September 19th. His son Scott brought his body home for burial and he was carried to his grave by six of his oldest employees wearing traditional white smocks.

To commemorate his life, an impressive plaque was erected in Arreton church, paid for by public subscription. *(above left)*

In Wellow's splendid Literary Institute a plaque and portrait commemorate the generosity of **James Preedy** (1840-1913) in redeeming an outstanding debt of £150.

Compared to Ruffin Blake with whom his path must have crossed, Preedy was an overner, retiring to Rossiters in Wellow with his wife Emma, his widowed father and two sons following a successful career as a London builder.

James's father Charles, a joiner, did sufficiently well to send him to Mr Clark's boarding school in Somerset before taking him into the family business. James married young and by 1871 he and Emma had four sons and two daughters.

At Wellow James became a pillar of the community and a member of Wellow Baptist Church, the first to be founded in the Island in 1801. Like many new brooms he was anxious to make innovations, being elected to the first Rural District Council and the County Council where he earned a reputation as an "advanced sanitarian." His promotion of hygiene had him labelled extravagant by the old timers who probably resented his new fangled ideas. He was sufficiently liked however to be elected to bodies as varied

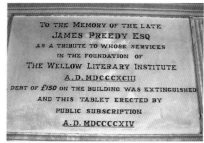

as the Asylum Committee, the Isle of Wight Smallholders Society, Calbourne Old Age Pensioners Committee and he was a trustee of the Yarmouth Ancient Order of Foresters.

James died in on November 9 1913 aged 73. His obituary reported that he was a "staunch radical" but not a "bigoted partisan." He and Emma are buried in the small burial ground at Wellow Baptist Chapel. *(opposite page, top right & this page, above)*

Child abuse has always shocked. When ten-year old **Valentine Gray** (1812-1822), a sweep's apprentice was found dead in an outhouse in Pyle Street Newport, his body covered in bruises and having received a fatal blow to the head, feelings rang high. His Master, a Mr Davis, and his wife were convicted of manslaughter.

Walking past Gray's Walk named in his memory, it is worth reflecting on the conditions prevalent at the time.

The Sweeps' Laws of 1788 stated that the minimum age for apprenticing such boys was eight and that a master should not send them up burning chimneys.

After Valentine's death, an Act of 1834 increased the minimum age of employment to ten years and by1840 it was increased to sixteen. It was not until 1875 that the Climbing Boys' Act prohibited the practice.

Young Valentine had been imported from Alverstoke in Hampshire. He was buried in Church Litten on January 5th 1822 and in death received recognition that he lacked in life, a monument paid for by public subscription being erected to mark his passing. *(page 102, full page)*

Surely the biggest fear of a seaman's wife is that her husband will drown? How hard then for Mrs Sivell whose husband **Thomas** (1721-1785) was shot by customs men who mistook him for a smuggler. Thomas, a ferryman, was plying his trade in the Solent when on June 15 1785 the accident happened. His tombstone in Binstead churchyard bears a warning to those who were responsible: *(page 104, top left)*

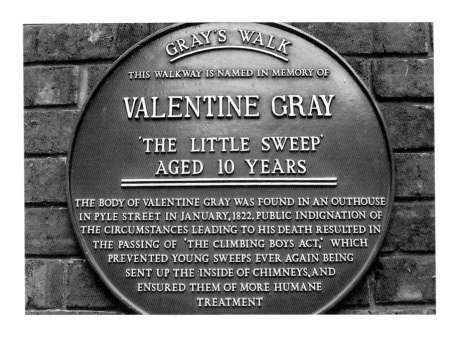

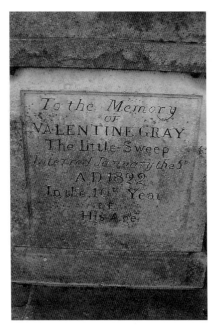

All you that pass pray look and see
How soon my life was took from me
By those officers as you may hear
They spill'd my blood that was so dear
But God is good and just and true
He will reward to each his due...

I wonder if they got their comeuppance?

A veritable dynasty of Hoffmeisters lie buried in Northwood Cemetery. The first to be interred was **Charles William Hoffmeister Esq.** Collector of Customs at Portsmouth and Belfast, born 1787, died 1869.

It was however medicine that defined the family's status. **Sir William Carter Hoffmeister**, along with his sons **William, George Bernard, John Bates and Henry Edgar** were all appointed Apothecary to Queen Victoria. Although their duties were restricted to the Queen's residence at Osborne, Sir William features in two royal photographs taken at Balmoral.

In 1900, William and Henry Edgar were both in practice as physicians and surgeons at Clifton House in Cowes. William was also medical officer and public vaccinator and certifying factory surgeon – a busy man.

Other male members of the family chose a naval career and the assembly of headstones at Northwood cemetery sport an interesting array of crosses, anchors and flowers as befitting the deceased. The last recorded death is that of Marion Emily, wife of William the surgeon who died at Cowes aged 85 in 1932.

Sometimes beautiful places are touched by tragedy. Walking east from Freshwater Bay towards Compton, a solitary obelisk bears witness to the sudden death of 15 year old **Edward Lewis Miller** (1831-1846), an only child who exhibited many proofs of great mental endowment, killed as he fell from the cliff while exploring on August 28 1846. The stark warning *"thou knowest not what the day may bring forth,"* is a sobering reminder of our mortality. Edward was returned to his home at Goudhurst in Kent for burial. *(page 104, top right)*

A similar tragedy took 14 year old **Francis Gray Bacon** (1877-1892) when on February 25th 1892 he was riding along the Undercliff. The Bacons moved to England from America after the death of their daughter, spending their summers at Ventnor. Frank's pony stumbled, he fell and his mother following in her carriage, witnessed the accident. Knocked unconscious he died two days later.

Frank was a brilliant child, fluent in Greek and Latin, writing history, hymns and poetry. His tutor wrote: "I have never met any boy who brought so much intellect to bear on his work." He is buried in Ventnor cemetery and a large block of Portland stone, encased in railings, marks the spot along the Undercliff where he died. *(opposite page, bottom left & bottom right)*

In 1852 Cowes boy **Freddie Attrill** was happily collecting shellfish on Osborne Beach when an obnoxious youth kicked over his bucket and told him to clear off. Freddie retaliated, landing a punch on the offending nose. Horrified adults intervened informing him that he had just assaulted the future king of England. Freddie was taken before the Queen but instead of execution or transportation, she commended him for standing up for himself. Henceforth, Freddie and shells became part of local history. In adulthood he decorated his house in Cambridge Road East Cowes with shells and in 2005, sculptor Glyn Roberts immortalised the event on a wall in Columbine Road. *(above left & right)*

Should we bite the bullet and prepare our own obituaries? A plaque in St Boniface tells us that **Thomas Prickett** (1781-1811), surgeon, *"with piety and resignation closed a life of extensive usefulness."* At St Helens, **Ellen Ellison** is praised as a paragon of virtue, *"The model of a Christian Wife and Woman,"* while in St Mildred's churchyard an inscription boasts how **John Broster** (1769-1862) at Edinburgh in 1823 discovered *"a system for the removal of impediments of speech."* Maybe a more modest commemoration would suffice, as with that of **Kenneth Hamilton Dalziel**, interred at Kingston Road, East Cowes whose contribution to life was that - *"He Tried"* - what more can one say?

Index of Names

Page

Page

Bibliography

Bowen: Marjorie, *Scandal of Sophie Dawes* *John Lane the Bodley Head, 1935*
Green: Margaret, = *Churches of the Isle of Wight,* *Winton Publications 1969*
Hiney: Tom, *On the Missionary Trail (biography of Daniel Tyerman)*
Hutchings: Richard J, *Alfred and Emily Tennyson: A marriage of True Minds*
Pub J W County Press 1991
Hyland: Paul, *Biography of an Island Dovecote Press*
Inwood: Stephen, *The Man Who Knew Too Much (biography of Robert Hooke)*
James: Rev Edward Boucher, *Letters Archaeological and Historical relating to the Isle of Wight*
(Vols 1 and II) Henry Frowde OUP 1896`
McKie: David = *Jabez, the Rise and Fall of a Victorian Rogue . Atlantic Books*
Ollard Richard, *Man of War (biography of Sir Robert Holmes) Hodder and Stoughton*
Phillips: Ken, *Shipwrecks of the Isle of Wight*
Phillips Kenneth S, *For Rooks and Ravens (the execution of Michal Morey)*
Isle of Wight Museum Publications
Summerson: John, *The Life and Works of John Nash . Allen and Unwin 1980*
Turley Raymond, *Isle of Wight Photographers 1840-1940 Southampton University*
Winter: CWR, *Manor Houses of the Isle of Wight Dovecote Press 1984*
Winter: Ron and Pat, *Village Churches of the Isle of Wight Forget-me-not Books 1987*
Wright: Dorothy, *Michael Hoy, the Man and his Monument Fernlea Publications 1992*

Other Sources

Dictionary of National Biography. *And* IW Family History Society web site
Ancestry web site. *And* Isle of Wight County Press. *And* Isle of Wight Public Record Office
Island Monuments web site to War Memorials (Geoff Allen). *And* Ventnor Heritage Centre

Acknowledgements and Special thanks to:

Geoff Allen, *re. the Gartside Tippings*
Rob Jennings *re. Elaine Anderson*
Peter Gaunt, university of *re. William Cromwell*
Mari Nicholson *re. James Ruffin Blake*
Tony and Wyn Daniell *re. Daniel Tyerman*
Fay Brown *re. John Hambrough/Francis Gray Bacon*
June Elford *re. John Dennett*
Dorothy Wright *re. Michael Hoy*
"Helen" - Isle of Wight County Press *re. use of archives*
Michael Hunter, English Heritage *re. Hughes/Mullins*
Tony Hayter, Wellow Literary Institute *re. James Preedy*